CODEPENDENT FREE

Stop Worrying About Others and Start Focusing on Yourself

JENNA BEATTIE

TABLE OF CONTENT

CODEPENDENT FREE

INTRODUCTION

The way to self-disclosure and recuperating can be tricky, particularly with regard to codependency. Codependency is a perplexing and guileful issue that can grab hold of our lives and keep us from arriving at our maximum capacity. It is an example of conduct wherein we become excessively enmeshed with the necessities and issues of others, forfeiting our own prosperity simultaneously. It can appear in associations with accomplices, relatives, companions, or even colleagues, and can have broad results on our psychological and profound well-being.

In any case, notwithstanding the difficulties, it is feasible to beat codependency and recover our lives. This book is a manual for that excursion, a far-reaching and empathetic assessment of the foundations of codependency and the means we can take to break free. Through a mix of individual stories, master bits of knowledge, and viable activities, we will dig into the idea of codependency, its impacts on our connections and self-awareness, and the methodologies we can use to recuperate and change our lives.

This is a book for anybody who has at any point felt caught in an example of codependency, for anybody who has attempted to keep up with sound limits or declare their requirements, and for any individual who is prepared to assume back command and fabricate a satisfying life. Whether you are simply beginning to perceive the indications of codependency or have been battling for quite a long time, this book is here to offer help, consolation, and direction. So assuming you are prepared to leave on the excursion of self-revelation and recuperating, how about we start?

CHAPTER ONE

Codependency

What it is & How It Happens

Codependency is quite possibly of the most well-known thing I work on with individuals in directing. I would sincerely figure that no less than 90% of individuals I find in treatment battle with some type of codependency. Odds are you've heard the word codependency previously, yet do you truly understand what it implies? The vast majority have some sort of regrettable underlying meanings related to the word. I would say, a many individuals focus on "ward", and think codependency implies that they are unreasonably poor and can't survive without a specific individual they're melded with. This can be what is going on in serious cases however

codependency all the more so alludes to an undesirable example of relating with others that will in general be exceptionally philanthropic.

Individuals who battle with codependency will generally place the requirements of others above them. They smother their own necessities in connections, feel awkward requesting things, and additionally say how they feel. It typically spins around an incorporated conviction that they are un-adorable as well as will be a weight to other people assuming that they request to have their requirements met or potentially straightforwardly express their feelings.

For what reason is it Called "Codependency"?

The word mutually dependent started with regard to AA and substance misuse treatment. It was said that the individual who is dependent on the substance is "reliant" on it. Any individual who has adored a fiend can let you know that it is exceptionally simple to get snagged into the show and mayhem that the enslavement causes. In these connections the individual who cherishes the fiend frequently winds up making facilities, overstretching themselves, and treading lightly to remain generally safe. The word codependency came around in light of the fact that the fiend is reliant upon the substance and the individual who loves them is subject to it as a substitute (mutually dependent). As it were, the individual who adores the fiend is impacted by the compulsion similarly as much as, while perhaps not more than the actual junkie. In the same way as other words utilized in brain research, the importance of the phrase codependency has developed throughout the long term and will in general interpretation with somewhat various implications relying upon the setting it is utilized in. Specific individuals use it to portray being excessively subject to an individual, being "dependent" on an individual, or even "dependent" on undesirable connections. Albeit these circumstances can positively be valid, the mutually dependent individual isn't guaranteed to see themselves as or look "subordinate" to someone else. I think it is more exact to portray the "reliant" as a piece of the word as implying that the individual's confidence and feeling of safety/security are subject to their connections with someone else and how that other individual feels. In this sense, codependency depends on the qualification between confidence and another regard. Confidence is the point at which you feel sure/alright/great about yourself since you realize you can deal with yourself and are by and large ready to finish things throughout everyday life. Another regard then again is the point at which your feeling of safety/worth/capacity is subject to your collaborations with others.

Confidence sounds like "I so much believe that I'm okay and have this under control". Another regard says "I really want to feel valuable/legitimate/great in your eyes to feel significantly better about myself". Somewhat this stuff is ordinary! All individuals experience some level of what may be marked codependency in connections, and that is great! It's the point at which it turns out to be excessively charitable that it turns into an issue when you're truly making a special effort and forfeiting to try not to disturb or burden someone else. Due to this disarray/obstacle on the word subordinate, there has been a push to rename codependency to "confidence deficiency jumble". This all the more satisfactorily mirrors the self versus other regard and nullifies the accentuation on unfortunate connections that are not generally present or the focal issue in codependency.

How Does Codependency Occur?

The main thing to comprehend about codependency is the way it works out. Codependency is basically a maladaptive adapting expertise that normally creates in youth. As kids brought up in unfortunate connections, this adapting ability is practical as it holds us protected back from being covered, disgraced, or generally squashed by undesirable guardians. When the kid grows up and leaves the undesirable climate, their mutually dependent ways of behaving will probably as of now not be utilitarian. The youngster no longer needs to appease their parents through mutually dependent ways of behaving, however by that point doing so has become imbued/programmed. The individual then pushes ahead applying those equivalent mutually dependent ways of behaving to future connections regardless of whether their accomplice isn't compromising/risky to them in the ways their parents were. Codependency then turns into an obstruction instead of an ability to survive. Understanding how codependency happens assists us with perceiving the reason why we act the manner in which we do and why those ways of behaving are at this point excessive.

Codependency doesn't necessarily need to come from being brought up in a family battling with enslavement. It normally happens in one of (or a blend of) 4 different ways:

- You were a parentified kid; meaning you were caused to feel liable for your folks as well as a family overall growing up, dealing with them rather than them dealing with you.
- You weren't permitted to be defective (each kid messes things up)
- You were disgraced or rebuffed for your feelings. The example here turns out to be that feelings drive friends and family away, as opposed to pulling them towards you in a steady manner.
- You were a casualty of gaslighting, which basically implies that your folks or other significant people refuted and made you question your feelings and insights to the point that you could have thought you were insane.

Any of these things or a blend of them can bring about an individual who conveys disgrace and the incorporated conviction that they are a weight. The saddest part about this that I find in treatment is that individuals who truly battle with codependency frequently need just to feel the closeness of good, good connections, however, they truly battle with simply being at the time and acting naturally when they are around others. Particularly individuals they care about. I frequently utilize this similarity: for the mutually dependent individual, expressing something such as "I don't have a solid sense of security and I really want you to hold me" or even something as straightforward as "no" can embrace a new lease on life would feel on the off chance that they were attempting to stumble into a road. In fact, you can make it happen… .yet there's a profound irritating sense in your stomach that you truly shouldn't and you'll probably get injured.

What might Advise Do With Codependency?

Directing for codependency spins around assisting individuals with investigating how they became mutually dependent, what it means for their ongoing connections, and how they can change their programmed mutually dependent ways of behaving. We do this through looking at and testing center suppositions like "I'm a weight assuming that I request help", and perceiving "triggers" that summon mutually dependent ways of behaving (a few triggers may be the possibility of requesting help or openness to saw or genuine struggle), perceiving programmed considerations that surface when you're setting off, and dealing with elective, more cognizant reactions to those triggers.

This could sound a little specialized and like something you could just peruse out of a book, and somewhat you can, yet guiding can be especially valuable in cases like this. Codependency rotates around feeling dangerous with individuals on a stomach level. It addresses a genuine break in an individual's capacity to have a solid sense of reassurance and agreement in connections. In guiding we work on codependency through the restorative relationship. I construct genuine, entrusting associations with my clients so they can feel alright with or potentially endure the transitory pressure of going up against their mutually dependent contemplations and ways of behaving with me. A large portion of the work occurs inside that relationship. Basically in codependency directing, I must resemble a sound parent. I will show up for you to help you, give genuine positive respect, and when you are unfortunate that you have a comment that could disturb me, I won't be that individual who gets annoyed and blows a gasket at you. Along these lines, you can investigate your codependency with some decrease in the trepidation/dread you feel from it, then get some experience being more decisive/helpless, then, at that point, apply it to different connections, and develop from that point. Cheerful, solid connections rely upon the capacity of every individual to be open to the next. Here and there this is frightening and awkward, however, you can't be close, associated, and secure without that weakness. This is particularly hard for individuals battling with codependency. A definitive objective of directing with regards to codependency is to reach a point where you are ready to be weak in a sound manner with individuals you love.

CODEPENDENT FREE

CHAPTER TWO

What Leads to Codependency

When individuals recognize that they have mutually dependent characteristics, they frequently start to ponder where these mutually dependent inclinations came from. For what reason are certain individuals defenseless to codependency in their grown-up connections? What causes codependency? For what reason is it so difficult to break free from mutually dependent connections?

While the responses aren't something very similar for everybody, for a great many people it starts in youth. This is significant on the grounds that kids are very naive. Small kids don't have the mental capacities or valuable encounters to understand that the connections they are seeing and encountering aren't sound; that their folk's arent in every case right; that guardians lie and control and come up short on abilities to give a protected connection.

Kids who experience childhood in useless families come to accept they don't matter or potentially they're the reason for the family issues

Broken families will generally have a portion of these qualities:

- Tumultuous and eccentric
- Unsupportive
- Frightening and dangerous
- Sincerely or potentially truly careless
- Manipulative
- Accusing
- Excessively brutal or harmful
- Disgracing
- Reject that the family has problems and decline outside help
- Cryptic
- Critical
- Absentminded
- Ridiculous assumptions for youngsters (anticipating that children should be great or get things done past what`s developmentally suitable)

The youngsters are faulted for the issues or are informed there isn't an issue (which is exceptionally confounding in light of the fact that the youngsters naturally know something is off-base, yet this feeling is never approved by the adults). The simplest way for youngsters to comprehend their tumultuous families is to pay attention to the pessimistic and contorted messages from grown-ups and expect "I'm the issue."

Accordingly, kids discover that they are awful, disgraceful, inept, unable, and the reason for the family's brokenness. This conviction framework makes the underlying foundations of grown-up mutually dependent connections.

At the point when guardians can't give a steady, strong, sustaining home climate, a few things can occur:

- You become a guardian. Assuming your parent was unequipped for satisfying the nurturing job, you might have taken on the nurturing role to fill in the holes. You took care of your parents or kin, covered the bills, prepared feasts, and kept awake to ensure

Mother didn't fall snoozing with a lit cigarette and torch the house.

- You discover that individuals who claim to cherish you may actually hurt you. Your life as a youngster experience was that family truly as well as sincerely hurt you, deserted you, misled you, undermined you, or potentially exploited your consideration. This turns into a recognizable dynamic and you let companions, darlings, or relatives keep on harming you in adulthood.

- You become an accommodating person. Keeping individuals cheerful is another way you try to feel in charge. You don't shout out or differ out of dread. You endlessly give. This feeds your self-esteem and gives you some profound satisfaction.

- You battle with limits. No one demonstrated sound limits for you, so yours are either excessively feeble (steady satisfying, and caretaking) or excessively inflexible (shut off and incapable to open up and trust others).

- You feel regretful. You most likely feel remorseful about a ton of things that you didn't cause. Among these things is your powerlessness to fix your folks or family. Despite the fact that it's unreasonable, there's a profound yearning to protect and fix it. What's more, your failure to change your family adds to your insecurities.

- You become unfortunate. The youth was frightened now and again. You didn't have the foggiest idea what was in store. Every so often went without a hitch, yet on different days you stowed away, stressed, and cried. Presently you keep on having sleep deprivation or bad dreams, feel anxious, and are reluctant about being distant from everyone else.

- You feel imperfect and shameful. You grew up feeling and additionally being informed that something is off about you. You came to accept this as truth since it was built up again and again when you didn't have a clue about some other reality.

- You have zero faith in individuals. Individuals have deceived and harmed you more than once. The outcome is that it's difficult to draw near and trust even your life partner or dear companions. This is your approach to shielding yourself from future hurt, but at the same time, it's a boundary to genuine closeness and association.

- You won't allow individuals to help you. You're not used to having your requirements met or having somebody deal with you. You're happier with giving assistance than getting it. You'd prefer to do it without anyone else's help then be obligated or have it utilized against you.

- You feel alone. For quite a while, you assumed you were the only one with a family like this or who felt like this. You felt alone and disgraced by the mysteries you needed to keep in adolescence. At the point when you consolidate this dejection with feeling apprehensive and defective, it's not difficult to see the reason why mutually dependent people will remain in broken connections as grown-ups as opposed to being separated from everyone else. Being separated from everyone else frequently feels like an approval that you are really imperfect and undesirable.

- You become excessively capable. As a kid, your endurance or your family's endurance relied upon you taking on liabilities that outperformed your age. You keep on being an incredibly trustworthy and mindful individual to the point that you might exhaust yourself and experience difficulty unwinding and having a good time. You likewise get a sense of ownership with others' sentiments and activities.
- You become controlling. At the point when life feels crazy and alarming, you overcompensate for your sensations of defenselessness by attempting to control individuals and circumstances.

In the event that you're mutually dependent, this is likely sounding intimately acquainted and maybe brings back some cherished, lifelong recollections.

Your experience growing up follows you into adulthood

You convey these relationship elements and irritating issues with you into your grown-up connections. Despite the fact that they're uninspiring, confounding, and startling, you rehash them since they're recognizable. You don't actually have the foggiest idea what a solid relationship is and you don't feel meriting one.

Be sympathetic to yourself

As a kid, you're stuck. You can't leave your family, so you track down ways of adapting. You foster procedures to get by. Thinking about your mutually dependent characteristics as versatile is an empathetic method for checking them out. They served you well as a kid. Presently you're a grown-up who can see the underlying foundations of your codependency all the more obviously. Your folks couldn't address your issues. This doesn't mean you're imperfect. You never again need to carry on with your life as a terrified kid who needs to demonstrate his/her value through each activity. Now is the ideal time to rise up out of that casing and be free. Requesting help is the initial step.

CHAPTER THREE

The Symptoms of Codependency

The term codependency has been around for very nearly forty years. In spite of the fact that it initially applied to mates of heavy drinkers, first called co-drunkards, research uncovered that the qualities of mutually dependent people were substantially more predominant in everyone than had been envisioned. As a matter of fact, they viewed that as assuming that you were brought up in a useless family or had an evil parent, almost certainly, you're mutually dependent. Try not to feel awful assuming that incorporates you. Most families in America are broken, so that covers pretty much everybody, you're in the greater part! They additionally found that mutually dependent side effects advanced in stages and deteriorated if untreated, however, the uplifting news was that they were reversible. Here is a rundown of the side effects. You shouldn't need to have every one of them to qualify as mutually dependent.

Disgrace and Low confidence

Not feeling that you're sufficient or contrasting yourself with others is an indication of low confidence. The precarious thing about confidence is that certain individuals respect themselves, yet it's just a cover for truly feeling detestable or lacking. Under, normally stowed away from awareness, are sensations of disgrace. A portion of the things that accompany low confidence is culpability sentiments and hairsplitting. In case everything is great, you won't regret it. (See my web journals on disgrace and hairsplitting.)

Individuals satisfying

It's fine to need to satisfy somebody you care about, yet mutually dependent people for the most part don't think they have a decision. Saying "No" causes them uneasiness. Some mutually dependent people struggle with saying "No" to anybody. They make a special effort and penance their own necessities to oblige others.

Unfortunate Limits

Limits are somewhat of a nonexistent line among you and others. It splits what's yours and another person's, and that applies not exclusively to your body, cash, and assets yet additionally to your sentiments, contemplations, and necessities. That is particularly where mutually dependent people cause problems. They have foggy or frail limits among themselves as well as other people. They feel liable for others' sentiments and issues or fault their own on another person.

Some mutually dependent people have unbending limits. They are cut off and removed, making it difficult for others to draw near to them. Now and then, individuals flip this way and that between having frail limits and unbending ones.

Reactivity

A result of unfortunate limits is that you respond to everybody's viewpoints and sentiments. You could think about things literally and get effortlessly set off. In the event that somebody says something you can't help contradicting, you either trust it or become protective. You retain their words since there's no limit. With a limit, you'd understand it was only their perspective and not an impression of you and you don't feel undermined by conflicts.

Caretaking

One more impact of unfortunate limits is that on the off chance that another person has an issue, you need to help them to the point that you could feel regretful in the event that you don't and surrender yourself all the while. It's normal to feel compassion and compassion toward somebody, however, mutually dependent people begin putting others in front of themselves. Truth be told, they need assistance and could feel dismissed on the off chance that someone else doesn't need assistance. Additionally, they continue to attempt to help and fix the other individual, in any event, when that individual plainly isn't taking their recommendation. For some mutually dependent people, their self-esteem is reliant upon being required.

Control

Control helps mutually dependent people have a solid sense of reassurance and security. Everybody needs some command over occasions in their day-to-day existence. You would have zero desire to live in steady vulnerability and disarray, yet for mutually dependent people, control restricts their capacity to face challenges and talk about their thoughts. Here and there they have a dependence that either assists them with relaxing, similar to liquor abuse or assists them in withholding their sentiments down, similar to workaholism so they don't feel crazy in cozy connections.

Mutually dependent people likewise need to control those near them, since they need others to act with a specific goal in mind to feel OK. As a matter of fact, human satisfaction and caretaking can be utilized to control and control individuals. Then again, mutually dependent people can be bossy and let others know what they ought to or shouldn't do. This is an infringement of another person's limit.

Broken correspondence

Mutually dependent people have inconveniences with regard to conveying their contemplations, sentiments, and necessities. Obviously, on the off chance that you don't have any idea about your thought process, feelings, or needs, this turns into an issue. At different times, you know, however, you won't take ownership of your reality. You're hesitant, to be honest on the grounds that you would rather not be furious with another person. Rather than saying, "I could do without that," you could imagine that it's OK or guide somebody. The correspondence becomes untrustworthy and befuddling when we attempt to control the other individual on account of our own trepidation.

Fixations

Mutually dependent people tend to invest their energy in pondering others or connections. Frequently, they attempt to unravel what another person is thinking or feeling and why. This is brought about by reliance on others and tensions and fears about being dismissed, because of disgrace. For a similar explanation, they can become fixated when they think they've made or could make a "botch."

Once in a while, you can pass into a dream about how you'd like things to be or about somebody you love as a method for keeping away from the aggravation of the present. This is one method for remaining willfully ignorant, talked about beneath, however, it holds you back from carrying on with your life.

Reliance

Mutually dependent people need others to like them to have an OK outlook on themselves, and they're apprehensive about being dismissed or deserted, in spite of the way that they can work all alone. Other mutually dependent people need to constantly be seeing someone, they feel discouraged or desolate when they're without help from anyone else for a really long time. This quality makes it difficult for them to cut off a friendship, in any event, when the relationship is excruciating or oppressive. They wind up feeling caught. Gain proficiency with the distinction between codependency and interdependency.

Forswearing

One of the issues individuals face in finding support for codependency is that they're trying to claim ignorance about it, implying that they don't deal with their concerns. Normally they often think the problem is someone else or the circumstance. They either continue griping or attempting to fix the other individual or move between various relationships or jobs and never own up to the way that they have an issue.

Mutually dependent people likewise deny their sentiments and necessities. Generally, they don't have any idea what they're feeling and are rather centered around the thing others are feeling. Exactly the same thing goes for their necessities. They focus on others' necessities and not their own. They may be trying to claim ignorance of their requirement for space and independence. Albeit some mutually dependent people appear to be penniless, others carry on like they're independent with regard to requiring help. They won't connect and experience difficulty getting in. They are trying to claim ignorance of their weakness and need for affection and closeness.

Issues with closeness

By this, I'm not alluding to sex, albeit sexual brokenness is in many cases an impression of a closeness issue. I'm looking at being open and close with somebody in a personal connection. In light of disgrace and frail limits, you could expect that you'll be judged, dismissed, or left. Then again, you might fear being covered by seeing someone lose your independence. You could deny your requirement for closeness and feel that your accomplice needs a lot of your time; your accomplice whines that you're inaccessible, yet the person is denying their requirement for separateness.

Agonizing feelings

Codependency makes pressure and prompts agonizing feelings. Shame and little self-esteem make uneasiness and flightiness about:

Being judged

Being dismissed or deserted

Committing errors

Being a disappointment

Being close and feeling caught

Being distant from everyone else

Each of the side effects leads to sensations of outrage and disdain, gloom, sadness, and despondency. At the point when the sentiments are excessive, you can feel numb.

CODEPENDENT FREE

CHAPTER FOUR

Steps of Codependency Recuperation

The general objective of codependency recuperation is to turn into a completely working person. That involves knowing, esteeming, and confiding in yourself, and putting yourself out there in your life and connections. It includes a total makeover that influences what you accept and your thought process, feelings, and acts.

Codependency untreated follows a similar constant, foundational decline as liquor abuse and a sickness — why some belief it to be an illness. The following is a framework of the movement of codependency side effects and indications of recuperation.

Beginning phase of Codependency and Recuperation

The beginning phase of codependency starts with becoming connected to someone else and closes with an undesirable reliance on that person. When you start recuperation, the beginning phase closes with starting to recover yourself.

The Infection Interaction

You may be drawn to a destitute individual or be excessively engaged with a relative and normally need to help or satisfy that person. Progressively, you become progressively sincerely subject to and fixated on that individual to the degree that you lose center around yourself and begin to surrender close companions and exercises.

The Beginning phase of Codependency

- Drawn to the destitute individual; offers assistance, gifts, dinners
- Endeavor to satisfy the individual
- Fixated on the individual and their way of behaving
- Justify and question your own discernments
- Refusal of codependency and habit or relationship issues, however, the concern develops
- Surrender your own exercises to accompany the individual
- Family and public activities impacted

- Progressively genuinely subject to the individual

The Recuperation Cycle

Emerging from disavowal implies you solidly face the issue and recognize reality as essential to evolving it. This shift may be propelled by another person's recuperation, by perusing this book, or more probably, it's set off an occasion — a reminder, alluded to as winding up in a seemingly impossible situation — that makes change basic. Rather than disregarding or limiting current realities, you remember them as troublesome and difficult, yet evident. You don't need to like them, yet you see them as they are.

Starting recuperation begins with getting data and connecting for help. By perusing this book, you've previously started looking for new responses and choices. Many individuals start psychotherapy or join a 12-step program, which gives them trust and starts the method involved with revamping their personality.

The Beginning phase of Recuperation

- Ends up in a very difficult situation and connects for help for their self
- Find out about codependency and enslavement
- Join a 12-step program or potential treatment
- Start to have trust
- Emerge from forswearing
- Learn recuperation is for self
- Pull together on self
- Start to fabricate your own personality

Center Phase of Codependency and Recuperation

The significant center phase of codependency and recuperation is where disavowal, difficult feelings, and over-the-top impulsive personal conduct standards are common. You increment your endeavors to control while learning about a greater amount of control. Once in recuperation, you recover freedom, balance, and more noteworthy true serenity.

The Illness Interaction

Without help, refusal and separation proceed, and issues deteriorate. You could limit and stow away from yourself as well as other people's difficult parts of your relationship and pull out from outside exercises and companions. In the meantime, your fixation on the relationship or enslavement and going with nervousness, hatred, and responsibility increment. You accomplish other things to help, empower, and control the other individual or the compulsion, and may try and assume control over their obligations. As emotional episodes and struggle increment, some mutually dependent people go to drugs, food, spending, or other habit-forming conduct to adapt.

Center Period of Codependency

- Deny/Cutoff anguishing portions of the relationship
- Hide away from others anguishing portions of the relationship
- Strain, obligation, and self-shortcoming augmentation
- Certainty reduces
- Pull out from outside friends and family
- Extended obsession with the individual or possibly oppression

- Endeavor to control by irritating, denouncing, criticizing, control
- Shock and disappointment due to broken ensures
- Scorn at frailty to control the person
- Perspective swings and extended battle and hostility
- Enable, oblige, and manage the other person's liabilities
- Disguise favored piece of data (subjugation, battle, social condition)
- Use food, alcohol, drugs, shopping, and work to adjust

The Recovery Collaboration

The middle stage is where a huge part of created by recovery occurs. You begin to practice non-detachment and handle your slightness over others and your obsession. As the consideration of yourself grows, so does self-commitment, care, and self-evaluation, which is significant for psychotherapy as well as 12-Step programs. AA underlines that a lush's flourishing relies upon careful self-reliability as the way to recovery.

This is similarly legitimate for commonly subordinate individuals and one of the 12 phases of CoDA, which are gotten from AA. Denouncing others and external circumstances denies your capacity to influence change and achieve bliss. Whether or not you're a loss from abuse, you track down the capacity to change your circumstances when the point of convergence of control shifts from the guilty party to yourself. Self-evaluation similarly consolidates overseeing youth gives that provoked your codependency.

In spite of the fact that knowledge of your way of behaving is important, it's deficient for change. Choices, activities, and hazard-taking are expected during the Center Stage. They happen when you're prepared and can't be constrained. It's difficult to change in any event, when you realize things would improve — like taking a superior work or moving to a positive region — however facing challenges where the result is dubious requires boldness — the mental fortitude to wander from the uneasiness that is recognizable into a new domain. This is one justification for why backing is fundamental.

During the center stage, you make new companions, partake in external exercises, and foster the capacity to be self-assured and defined limits. As you become all the more genuinely free, you care more for yourself, and reactivity, empowering, and controlling ways of behaving decrease.

Center Phase of Recuperation

- Figure out feebleness
- Mindfulness develops
- Start dependence on an otherworldly source
- Start to withdraw
- Make new companions
- Foster external exercises
- Quit empowering and controlling
- Figure out how to be emphatic
- Get a sense of ownership of yourself
- Increment taking care of oneself and confidence
- Put down stopping points and less receptive
- More close-to-home autonomy
- Recuperate adolescence wounds

Late-Phase of Codependency and Recuperation

In the late phase of codependency and recuperation, the difference between illness and well-being is generally articulated. The untreated mutually dependent's reality has been fundamentally restricted and their degrees of well-being and working have seriously declined, while the recuperated mutually dependent's reality has extended to incorporate more serious gamble-taking, connections, and new objectives.

The Sickness Interaction

As sickness advances, outrage and clashes are more normal, and confidence and taking care of oneself further decay. Sadness, void, and despondency win. The ongoing pressure of codependency appears in new side effects, for example, stress-related medical issues and new or further developed fanatical habitual ways of behaving and addictions. These ways of behaving and addictions could remember customary checking for the junkie, issues, empowering, cleaning the house, counting calories, working out, spending, or utilizing lawful or unlawful medications.

Late Phase of Codependency

This is the movement of codependency in the late stage on the off chance that you sit idle.

- Foster's actual side effects
- Feel furious, miserable, and discouraged
- Over the top urgent way of behaving, addictions
- Further decrease in self-regarded
- Gloom and absence of taking care of oneself
- Expanded clashes

The Recuperation Interaction

In the late phase of recuperation, your confidence and certainty return. You're enabled to seek after your own objectives and are more broad, innovative, and unconstrained. You want to put yourself out there for the sheer happiness and opportunity of it completely. As your center moves from somebody outside yourself, you completely comprehend that your joy doesn't rely on others and never again have an urgent should be seeing someone. Simultaneously, you want and are fitter for legitimate closeness.

Late Phase of Recuperation

These are the prizes you procure assuming you stay with recuperation.

- Joy doesn't rely on others
- Confidence and certainty return
- Have own power and seek after objectives
- Are far-reaching, inventive, unconstrained
- Encounters confidence and self-sustaining
- Appreciate interdependency and closeness

Recuperation from codependency requires progressing upkeep in or out of a relationship. For this reason, individuals go on in 12-Step programs even after they've abandoned a fiend or enslavement. Solely after various years do the progressions and instruments of recuperation and well-being become pieces of you.

CODEPENDENT FREE

CHAPTER FIVE

Overcoming Codependency

Saving Your Relationship

Solid connections comprise the two players compromising, while codependency is a poisonous pattern of one individual providing for what feels required. The other individual is a taker and permits their accomplice to offer without getting anything as a trade-off.

In the event that you are searching for a method for saving your relationship, this guide might be exactly the thing you've been searching for. We will make sense of what a mutually dependent relationship is, and how to beat codependency.

What is codependency?

At the point when one individual forfeits their own necessities and maintains that all together should serve another person, they are considered mutually dependent.

Here the provider imagines that they are forfeiting their requirements since another person needs them to do as such. They should be required.

Codependency inside a heartfelt connection whether you are dating wedded, or in the middle between, adds power to the circumstance since you are sincerely involved.

We acknowledge activities like codependency as a typical way of behaving in light of the fact that we stunt ourselves into imagining that we are doing it for somebody that we care about. This additionally makes us imagine that they need us to keep acting along these lines.

Goal Requires A Smidgen Of Soul Looking

Self-acknowledgment can be very testing. Frequently it isn't until you have a severe shock, or get tired of the status quo that you need to roll out an improvement.

On the off chance that you are perusing this book, right now is an ideal opportunity to be totally transparent with yourself regarding what heading your center has taken. Give yourself a minute to ask yourself, "Does this define me in this relationship?"

This isn't an opportunity to fault yourself, yet to just recognize what you will permit in your space. To perceive what you probably shouldn't permit from here on out.

Compulsion and Codependency

Could it be said that we are dependent on being required? Do we throw our own necessities to the side due to our dependence on being required?

Compulsion doesn't necessarily in all cases allude to a substance like medications or liquor. It can likewise relate to a cerebrum issue that makes us urgently rehash activities due to the prize or the inclination and boosts connected to it.

Codependency and our dependence on it are extremely real factors to confront. It tends to be harmful to the two sides. So whether you are the provider or the taker and you need to mend together, it is critical to recognize the truth about it. A few normal pointers are:

- Feeling frantic to please.

- Fixation on giving or satisfying.
- Never having space. A should be together constantly.

Feeling caught in a sensational and controlling relationship. (This can apply to the two individuals.)

In the event that any of these situations fit you, it very well may be a sign you are in a poisonous relationship. You might have never thought about it because of the pattern of codependency keeping you locked in.

What is a harmful relationship and how would we perceive that we are in one?

The most effective method to Conquer Codependency in A Harmful Relationship

Being in a poisonous relationship fundamentally implies that it is undesirable and is definitely not an equivalent organization that is supporting those that are in it.

One detailed story sign that a relationship is harmful is that it is all "take", and negative "give".

At the point when you penance your requirements to provide for your accomplice, it gives the sense you are forfeiting your relationship, however, there is no equilibrium, leaving you feeling undervalued and most frequently, depleted.

Frequently, we won't remember it ourselves. We are not generally legitimate with ourselves when we are in an unfortunate circumstance, particularly assuming we are genuinely contributing. This can relate to companions, darlings, youngsters, and guardians. No relationship is absolved. We should be tireless in taking care of ourselves and perceiving what genuinely harms us is critical.

Parting ways with Codependency

Codependency is a hazardous propensity to clutch. At the point when we understand that we are caught in a pattern of undesirable ways of behaving we can begin to address them and track down the fitting treatment to assist with directing our emotional wellness. This is vital. Not just in this last endeavor to save our relationship, but more significantly in saving ourselves from specific brokenness.

Presently this is a lot not exactly simple or easy. As a manual for a better you, here are a few successful tips to begin your excursion.

The first and potentially most significant step is perceiving and recognizing there is an issue of some kind or another. Codependency won't disappear all alone. It is generally connected to an underlying issue either on the provider's side or with the two accomplices. Obviously, you can separate, yet it won't determine the basic issue.

Since the issue won't disappear assuming that the relationship closes, it just has passed on to rehash the same thing in later connections. This will go on until the provider begins to define better limits.

Treatment can assume a significant supporting part in mending from the underlying issue to codependency. Conversing with an expert that is prepared to assist individuals with relationship endlessly issues from the past is only a call away. A few famous and demonstrated treatments include:

EDMR Treatment

Talk treatments (psychotherapy) are a delicate yet compelling and exhaustive method for treating injury and the problems they have made in our lives. One method for treating codependency is EDMR.

EDMR represents Eye Desensitization and Going back over. In this treatment, you will discuss and go up against subdued recollections and pictures, managing them next to each other with your advisor.

An expert separates this treatment into stages. Contingent upon the special circumstances, a leap forwards might take a few meetings.

Does EDMR Work In One Meeting?

EDMR doesn't work in that frame of mind for anybody. However, codependency won't be restored with one meeting of any treatment and that ought to recognize before starting. This requires some investment, however, the time is all around spent and compensated eventually.

Multi-meeting medicines are particularly valid for codependency that has been framed from a past horrendous encounter.

Does EDMR work for codependency assuming that it is established in injury?

Indeed, EDMR takes care of business for those that have had to deal with awful encounters. The specialist will accept meetings as leisurely and tenderly on a case-by-case basis to deal with a serious injury. This sort of treatment is turning out to be increasingly more pursued as emotional well-being marks of shame corrupt.

Gathering or Couples Treatment

Many individuals decide to look for treatment for their codependency through individual meetings. However, going as a couple can end up being extremely gainful. This course is for those who decide to fix and mend together. This isn't ideal for everybody and that is Totally fine.

Couples treatment will assist the two accomplices with understanding the pattern of codependency, it is no attempt at finger-pointing to guarantee there. This can be exceptionally compelling assuming the two individuals are prepared to accomplish the work and change together.

Different treatments to address codependency.

The best sorts of treatment center around ways of behaving and transforming them in a positive manner.

Converse with an expert about your choices for guiding now that you realize you are not kidding about assuming command. Regardless of whether you choose to push ahead together, you will acquire from learning knowledge.

Meanwhile, you can help yourself by:

- Being aware of your circumstance and your activities. Wonder why you answer with no response.
- Be caring to yourself. Take a moment to remind yourself that you're giving it your all.
- Keep cool-headed and centered. Contemplation and careful breathing will send your cerebrum the oxygen it requires to obviously think.
- Encircle yourself with individuals who carry worth to your life.

Laying out Sound and Sensible Limits

The principal part or deficiency in that department, codependency flourishes with its limits. At the point when we don't have sound limits set up to show others our limits, these lines are many times crossed placing you in an awkward spot. These cutoff points are set up to safeguard your psychological and actual well-being and are a vital perspective in solid connections.

Limits are not set to hurt others. It will prevent them from exploiting you. In the event that it appears to be frightful to them, you can look at this as a warning. Out of appreciation for the advanced age express, "Treat others as you need to be dealt with", regarding these limits will set the groundwork of your relationship.

Having some time off

While an individual is going through treatment to treat their codependency, they might find it supportive to have some time off from their relationship or accomplice. Recuperating from injury appears to be unique for everybody and may be finished all alone.

This doesn't mean getting a separation on the off chance that you are hitched or settling on any serious choices right now. A break just gives you the distance between the circumstance that you are attempting to manage.

A break can provide you with an alternate perspective on your way of behaving and the operations of your relationship to obviously see things more. Enjoying some time off can, in itself, help to break the pattern of codependency.

Bliss Comes From The Inside

Helping other people is an incredible method for giving fulfillment and joy to our lives, as well as theirs. It is the point at which we start to disregard ourselves and our necessities that it crosses a limit from aiding them to harming ourselves. This turns into an extremely undesirable type of giving joy to our lives.

At the point when we have interior joy, we signal self-confidence to show others the regard we hope to be shown.

Inward satisfaction is an excursion. It could remember tracking down another reason for life, having an uplifting outlook, or making space in your day to zero in on yourself and your development. It doesn't make any difference. It just has to fulfill you.

Comprehend That Nonappearance Causes The Heart To become Fonder

One side effect of codependency is waiting to be a major piece of another person's life. Wanting to associate with somebody such a lot of gives you no chance to miss them.

Regardless of whether we are not around that individual without fail, we invest the majority of our significant investment contemplating them or doing stuff for them.

This isn't adoring, this is a fixation. What's more, it shows that we are dependent on the inclination that we get from them requiring us or requiring us to get things done for them.

Having your limits set up and breaking the pattern of continually being associated with your accomplice will demonstrate that nonattendance causes the heart to become fonder. This thusly can really reinforce your relationship and extend your affection for each other.

Try not to Think about it Literally

At the point when your accomplice starts to split away from the pattern of codependency and begins to do the things on their own that you once accomplished for them, don't think about it literally or fly off the handle.

They really do in any case require you as an accomplice. We can figure out how to get things done all alone and learning assists us with developing.

View it as them developing. Be pleased with them, and glad for them as opposed to imagining that they never again need you.

On the other side, on the off chance that you are mutually dependent, attempt to offer yourself a reprieve. Partaking in your time, rehearsing, and taking care of yourself while resting your brain. Indulge yourself in satisfying yourself!

Center Around Yourself

Relieving codependency incorporates moving the concentration from your accomplice to yourself. It will require exertion and investment to figure out how to zero in on yourself, yet you will feel improved when you do.

Rather than relying upon others to cause you to feel needed, required, and approved, you will before long begin to....

Pick Yourself.

For some individuals, a mutually dependent relationship isn't their most memorable involvement in showing codependency. This might be a long-lasting trademark.

Many individuals battle with this in light of the fact that as a kid they acted this way with their folks or kin, getting positive or negative fortifications. Others might be shaky or have over their lifetime, been ignored inwardly. Wanting to be required comes in many structures, all similarly legitimate and having the right to determine.

Fostering Your Own Side interests

In giving such a huge amount to someone else we can neglect to focus on what our own advantages are. What are a few leisure activities that you once had but have quit participating in readily?

The time has come to reach out with things that interest you and carry enhancement and satisfaction to your life.

Ideal Relationship Wellbeing

What does a solid relationship resemble starting now and into the foreseeable future? Furthermore, how frequently does a relationship endure going from codependency to mending and solid functions?

The answer to this is is quite different for every individual.

Going through outrageous changes and by will continuously significantly affect a relationship. This is particularly valid for something like codependency, which is changing the individual yet in addition straightforwardly influences the elements of the relationship.

Eventually, you will both know your own cutoff points as well as your accomplices and will ideally decide to similarly regard them. On the occasion, you decide to go your various ways you will have more deeply studied yourself and what you really want in this life.

Figure out how To Be Content Without help from anyone else

One more explanation that we could stick to our codependency as firmly as we do is that we are awkward with being without anyone else or being distant from everyone else.

We could feel that continually providing for somebody will keep them from requiring us. We keep them around so we don't need to support the vibe of being desolate.

So here's something to challenge you....

Something you might not have pondered in some time is what your necessities and needs are. Shut your eyes and truly ponder that briefly.

Presently go satisfy them. No justifiable reasons. Simply go make it happen. You merit it and you are worth the effort.

Saving Your Relationship

For a relationship to go from undesirable to solid and endure it requires devotion and exertion from the two accomplices. It likewise takes genuineness and eagerness to concede where there were past shortcomings.

Codependency is a harmful relationship characteristic. When we get away from things that were poisonous to us we can start to recuperate. So is it conceivable to rescue this disaster area we've made?

Obviously. There is generally space for genuine affection.

CODEPENDENT FREE

CHAPTER SIX

Codependent Marriage

It tends to be challenging to decide if you are in a mutually dependent marriage. All things considered, nobody needs to look for issues in their relationship. Notwithstanding, in the event that you are in a marriage that may be considered mutually dependent, it is ideal to recognize it and do whatever it may take to forestall further issues.

Most importantly, you should comprehend what codependency is in a marriage. Codependency alludes to a close-to-home and social condition where somebody is excessively subject to the next individual to satisfy fundamental necessities. The easiest definition is being dependent on someone else to an unfortunate end.

Some say that it is like being dependent on your accomplice. In spite of motion pictures and romance books telling the overall population that this is a sweet signal and implies that the adoration is colossal, being dependent on a mate is staggeringly undesirable and can become risky. Assume you have arrived where you are uncertain in the event that this is your relationship, and assuming you really want marriage help, it tends to be more clear to you assuming you know a precisely exact thing a mutually dependent relationship involves.

Many variables can contribute to and prompt codependency in connections. The ongoing Symptomatic and Factual Manual of Mental Issues (DSM 5-TR) depicts subordinate behavioral condition as a drawn-out condition in which somebody has an unreasonable should be dealt with and can't take care of their own necessities independently. Notwithstanding, codependency can exist without this issue or can cover with other psychological maladjustments. Living with psychological instabilities or behavioral conditions can influence the manner in which somebody connects with others. For instance, somebody with a marginal behavioral condition might encounter serious emotional episodes and an absence of profound control which might possibly influence their relationship elements.

These side effects can be made do with an emotionally supportive network, for example, counseling psychological well-being experts. Emotional well-being America is a non-benefit that teaches individuals about psychological well-being conditions and assists people with finding assets they might require. These are only a portion of the manners in which individuals can attempt to beat issues with codependency and deal with their psychological wellness all the more real.

Sexual maltreatment is another model that might possibly prompt mutually dependent propensities and make a power unevenness between accomplices. No one ought to be dependent upon this kind of conduct and there are assets accessible to help them.

There are circumstances where one accomplice or family might depend on one more without it being considered personal codependence. For instance, brief or long haul actual sickness might keep somebody from dealing with themselves completely, needing actual help from a mate. Nonetheless, this doesn't innately connote a profound reliance or relationship habit.

Could it be said that you are In A Mutually dependent Marriage?

What does codependency resemble in a marriage? Marriage is a legitimately official agreement between two grown-ups. At the point when a grown-up can't genuinely or mentally handle their own necessities, they are mutually dependent. The mutually dependent life partner can't go with choices autonomously, depending on the other to make their dinners, and could try and need them monetarily.

While there are special cases for the standard, numerous mutually dependent relationships display a few signs. A solitary mark of codependency isn't commonly worried until additional variables become an integral factor. A mutually dependent marriage will probably incorporate the accompanying qualities:

- The failure to appropriately convey
- Neglect to see the codependency
- Separation anxiety
- Needs the endorsement of others
- Battles with direction

- Low confidence
- Incapable to track down satisfaction without your accomplice
- Surrendering your own wellbeing
- Steady sensations of nervousness
- Assuming your accomplice's liability

While a portion of the previously mentioned variables can be free of codependency, a great deal of them could indicate being engaged in a mutually dependent marriage. Having a more noteworthy comprehension of every potential trademark will explain the purposes for everyone and the way things are associated with codependency.

The failure to appropriately convey

Attempting to convey in a marriage can create a ton of issues. Correspondence issues can originate from a few things, one of which is codependency. Somebody who is mutually dependent is frequently excessively frightened to disturb their accomplice, so fair and open correspondence isn't fundamentally important. All things being equal, a mutually dependent relationship will encourage a propensity for incorporating pessimistic sentiments.

Containing sentiments isn't great for any relationship and will bring on some issues in a drawn-out relationship like a marriage. In light of the apprehension about rankling, disheartening, or in any event, confounding a mutually dependent accomplice, numerous things ought to be examined or gotten to the next individual's consideration of the relationship. Staying away from any issues has an approach to developing over the long run, not a great explanation behind the unfortunate correspondence.

Neglect to see the codependency

A marriage wherein one or two people are mutually dependent is in many cases one that neglects to perceive how mutually dependent they really are. For pariahs, a mutually dependent marriage may be self-evident. In any case, those in the marriage frequently accept that their way of behaving is ordinary. It could take the marriage counselor of others to bring up the expected issue in a mutually dependent marriage.

Separation anxiety

Surrender is a typical trepidation with regard to a mutually dependent relationship. This dread can influence numerous ways of behaving in the marriage, from wanting to get consent to do straightforward things to being extraordinarily tenacious. Being abandoned or deserted is the main thrust behind a ton of mutually dependent individual activities.

Needs the endorsement of others

Codependency makes a longing in individuals to have the endorsement of others. This is particularly valid for the mate of the mutually dependent person. Getting their approval is really important for somebody that battles with their own picture. Satisfying their life partner turns into a need over doing what fulfills them.

Battles with direction

At the point when it is difficult for a grown-up to pursue their own choices and surrender them to their accomplice, codependency is logical. For instance, the powerlessness to pick something basic, similar to what they ought to wear that day, or spend an extra $10 on. This is frequently due to the mutually dependent individual depending on their accomplice to go with every one of the choices. Leaving all the decision-production to a solitary individual in a marriage is an indication that codependency is available.

Low confidence

A person that considers modest themselves might join themselves to someone else. At the point when an individual with low confidence feels required by the other individual, they depend on their accomplice for that vibe. Assuming that that sensation of need was to vanish, a mutually dependent individual would probably confront a much more unfortunate sensation of uselessness. At the point when a relationship has arrived at that point - where one party feels useless without the other - obviously, a mutually dependent marriage is available.

Incapable to track down satisfaction without your accomplice

At the point when an individual's satisfaction is totally reliant upon their mate, codependency is an enormous piece of the relationship. On the off chance that one individual in the marriage should leave town on a work trip, the mutually dependent individual left behind may be hopeless while their mate is no more. Missing your life partner while they are away is ordinary however battling to work due to the sensation of being inadequate is a glimmering sign of codependency.

Surrendering your own wellbeing

Frequently, a husband or wife in a mutually dependent marriage will forfeit their own well-being and health to give all they have to the mutually dependent life partner. This could mean arriving at elevated degrees of stress and nervousness to guarantee that their life partner is very actually liked. For instance, a life partner who quits going to their week-by-week exercise class to ensure that their mutually dependent other half eats is a penance normal for a mutually dependent marriage.

Steady sensations of nervousness

A mutually dependent marriage is frequently loaded up with nervousness. The restless inclination could come from being away from each other while at work or doing. It could likewise come from the uneasiness of not understanding what you could do in the event that your life partner at any point left you or died. While those contemplations may be a far-off worry to anybody in a marriage, in the event that it causes consistent uneasiness, marriage help might be essential.

Assuming your accomplice's liability

By and large, the term mutually dependent marriage was held for those in a marriage with a junkie life partner. At the point when you have a husband or wife with a medication or liquor compulsion, numerous mates feel they are helping by empowering the way of behaving. Empowering is many times done by assuming the obligations of the fiend. For instance, they could cancel when they can't come to attempt to save their work. While this is the worker's liability, a mate that does this is probable in a mutually dependent marriage.

Is Help Important In A Mutually dependent Marriage?

You could consider what is so terrible about a mutually dependent marriage. Aren't individuals seeing someone to rely upon each other? Aren't families expected to help each other? To a degree, yes: contingent upon your accomplice is essential for seeing someone. Nonetheless, there is a line that should be drawn and sound limits that should be laid out. An excessive amount of dependence on someone else can demolish one's healthy identity. They never again exist as 'me.'

Looking for help when you are in a mutually dependent marriage is many times a vital stage to finding yourself once more. The strain that is placed on the less reliant individual could truly hurt in various ways. Likewise, the possibility that one individual should give such a huge amount to their companion can push the less reliant individual to leave the relationship. Not exclusively is the finish of marriage not great, yet additionally, it will be extraordinarily challenging for the mutually dependent person.

Marriage guidance for mutually dependent people is accessible to those out of luck. For some, directing is the most ideal choice. An instructor or specialist has the devices accessible to help the mutually dependent turn out to be more independent and surer of themselves. Directing can likewise help the companion of a mutually dependent person to figure out how to lead their accomplice in separating a little at a time. The objective of a mutually dependent marriage looking for help is to permit every individual to turn into their own individual again while figuring out how to be in a solid marriage.

Figuring out how to supplant mutually dependent ways of behaving with a solid, caring way of behaving can be a difficult yet conceivable excursion. With help from a certified proficient, you could track down your approach to conquering codependency and accomplishing a commonly fulfilling relationship. Experts are prepared to assist with breaking the pattern of useless connections by supporting you to assume command over your own sentiments and your own way of behaving. Research has demonstrated the treatment to be a successful device in restricting mutually dependent propensities in connections.

Looking for help is much of the time the best move that a wedded couple can initiate before things heighten. For a union to be sound, codependency ought to be restricted. Couples treatment can be an incredible method for finding the help you really want.

CODEPENDENT FREE

CHAPTER SEVEN

Becoming Less Codependent In Any Relationship

It's difficult to be seeing someone not want to be excessively associated with your accomplice's life, however it can create issues for the two players if you don't watch out. In spite of the fact that it tends to be challenging to perceive while you're being mutually dependent, particularly in the event that you're not used to being distant from everyone else and not managing things all alone, there are ways of turning out to be less mutually dependent in your relationship.

In a mutually dependent relationship, you keep an eye on the necessities of the other individual and are seen as the 'provider' in the relationship and when you don't feel required by the other individual, you will generally feel useless and miserable. In spite of that is the empowering agent who is seen as the 'taker.' They will keep on taking from the provider.

This kind of relationship frequently becomes undesirable and is built up over the long run. Albeit these connections are frequently undesirable and are not supportable long haul there are ways you become less mutually dependent in your relationship.

Indications of a mutually dependent relationship

- It's a broken relationship. Both of you feel they can't exist without each other. Being mutually dependent makes a round relationship where one individual requires the other individual who then needs their accomplice to be required.

This is exceptionally unfortunate and is supported over the long haul, by the two individuals. This likewise makes a relationship that has undesirable correspondence and where one individual requires the other individual who then should be required.

- There is unfortunate personal holding. Individuals in mutually dependent connections at times experience the ill effects of close-to-home holding. You are both so sincerely joined to one another that you can't work without one another regardless of whether this connection isn't solid or really great for both of them.

- There is an awkwardness of force. This happens when one individual is giving a lot of energy and time to the relationship with an over-the-top spotlight on the other individual. This individual frequently will exploit this - frequently accidentally. This will in general boost their necessities and wants to spurn the other individual's requirements and wants.

- You need to transform them. At the point when we understand our accomplice is unique in relation to us, frequently in basic ways, we should transform them so the distinctions and frequently the struggle is less. This won't ever work. An individual can change in the event that they need to. Trying to change someone is an impossible journey to embark on.

- Your absence of taking care of oneself. You neglect how you need to hang out. There may be things you need to do, however, don't do them since you need to invest energy in them. Investing energy with your accomplice is great and can be solid - inside sound cutoff points and limits. It very well may be difficult for you to completely finish designs that you made when you understand you will part ways.

- You can't portray your relationship. At the point when you are in a mutually dependent relationship, you could struggle with making sense of or sharing your considerations and sentiments about the relationship. This is frequently in light of the fact that you are hyper-centered around the other individual and unfit to explain how you truly feel.

- You struggle with being distant from everyone else. Being mutually dependent frequently brings about you struggling with enduring being distant from everyone else or not hearing from your accomplice. Being distant from everyone else causes you to feel disrupted and restless.

- Your necessities are not being met. This is frequently in light of the fact that you battle to request what you really want. Some of the time you don't know what you want or on the grounds that you are - once more - so centered around the other individual, you don't have the foggiest idea what you want. Additionally, regardless of whether you understand what you want, you believe you don't reserve the privilege to request what you really want.

How Can Somebody Become Mutually dependent?

Codependency is in many cases established in unfriendly youth encounters (Expert). You have become mutually dependent when you took on an improper close-to-home liability or you were 'parentified' (being put in a parental job quite early on) to endure a horrendous childhood.

At the point when this happens you figured out how to disregard and neglect your requirements for your folks.

Sadly, this turns into a learned way of behaving that from one viewpoint assisted you with enduring your experience growing up, yet put you in a position to battle to keep up with solid connections as a grown-up. And time after time, your parent is either finished or defensive which empowers in undesirable ways for the youngster to become mutually dependent.

Yet, having mindfulness and comprehension of codependence can assist you with finding lucidity and harmony in your connections, which can be the way to being less mutually dependent. Remember - change IS conceivable.

You Might Be In a Mutually Dependent Relationship If:

- You feel restless on the off chance that you don't hear from your accomplice.
- You are too destitute in the relationship.
- You struggle with being without them for broadened timeframes. You really want to continually see and hear from them.
- Your relationship is the wellspring of your general satisfaction, self-esteem, and confidence.
- You experience a consistent feeling of dread toward dismissal, surrender, and analysis.
- You generally want to guarantee they are content with you.

- You don't have the foggiest idea how to deal with yourself without them there to help.
- You frequently attempt to change your accomplice since you clutch an excessively glorified perspective on your accomplice.
- Issues stay progressing and neglected amplified by unfortunate correspondence and a relationship unevenness
- You feel like you can't survive without them.
- You feel a powerful urge to keep yourself associated with the other individual.

Hints On the most proficient method to Turn out to be Less Mutually dependent in Your Relationship

It's normal for individuals in connections to become mutually dependent. It's a characteristic inclination that we as a whole have. It's not really something terrible except if there is a lopsidedness of force and you spurn your requirements for someone else.

Notwithstanding, there are ways you can begin to mend and turn out to be less mutually dependent

Figure out how to put your own requirements first

Take a moment to question yourself, what is valuable to me? How is something that I might want to respond to that addresses my issues? These are significant inquiries since when an individual becomes mutually dependent, they can without much of a stretch lose their healthy identity - like what their identity is and what they need. It's essential to be egotistical on occasion. Find these times with the goal that you can respect your necessities and needs. This assists you with turning out to be less sincerely penniless.

It's critical to figure out how to deal with yourself before you can help other people do likewise. This implies ensuring that your essential requirements are met and that your sentiments are approved by another person in your mind as well as without holding back.

At the point when you can begin to deal with yourself, you are less inclined to experience physical, mental, or close-to-home issues. It is frequently trying for you to put yourself first, yet this is a basic initial step.

Practice taking care of oneself

Taking care of oneself can be anything you need it to that sustains you in truly, inwardly, and intellectually sound ways. This could be washing up or going for a run. It could likewise mean gathering with companions or partaking in side interests that give pleasure into your life - like composition, journaling, perusing - simply any movement or leisure activity - without your accomplice.

This implies figuring out how to esteem yourself and find and honor your own necessities. Journaling is an incredible method for showing self-esteem and composing ways you can confirm yourself. Taking care of oneself additionally implies precisely the exact thing it says - care for yourself - anything that this might seem to be. This likewise assists you with turning out to be less angry with your accomplice.

Speak with your accomplice

The main thing you can do to make your relationship better is to begin speaking with your accomplice. In the event that you don't speak with your accomplice about what makes the person in question cheerful or miserable, you will not be able to offer the help fundamental for development and improvement.

Figure out how to communicate your requirements, tune in with aim, and find new manners by which you can begin to speak with your accomplice in additional compelling and solid ways.

Great correspondence likewise incorporates being confident (utilizing your voice, not being forceful) saying the way that you feel utilizing 'I' proclamations, and acting with thought and understanding.

Begin speaking with your accomplice which intends that assuming you are approached to accomplish something this evening and you are not capable, then say I'm not accessible right now instead of giving a reason. This additionally implies imparting to your accomplice the underlying foundations of your codependency and your longing to change. Better correspondence assists you with being more sure utilizing your voice and roll out important improvements.

Individuals who are mutually dependent on connections frequently convey their requirements in a detached forceful manner, filled with hatred, juvenile and crude (thinking and acting), and coming up short of a healthy identity.

Distinguish designs in your day-to-day existence

Ponder the examples in your day-to-day existence and what they mean for your accomplice. For instance, assuming you will more often than not get exceptionally restless before huge occasions or when things are evolving rapidly, consider what this could mean for your accomplice.

They also might be having a restless outlook on plans changing without a second to spare or on the other hand in the event that they have something upsetting happening at work. It's vital to comprehend what your activities mean for one another with the goal that you can uphold each other in the midst of hardship.

Likewise critical to distinguish the triggers that actuate your requirements to deal with others and satisfy others, neglecting your identity.

It likewise assists with distinguishing designs in your day-to-day existence that drove you to become mutually dependent and to likewise find opportunities to find and search for indications of being in a solid relationship. You can do this by disentangling your examples as well as by taking a gander at consolidating new examples of relating.

Inquire: Am I this way in different connections? Or on the other hand in past close connections? This is an ideal opportunity to do a relationship stock to sort out your examples.

Dive more deeply into codependency

Turning out to be more mindful is the initial step and afterward find the following way to learn about codependency to teach yourself and become more proficient. This will likewise assist you with evolving.

Past finding out about codependency, additionally read about injury and your connection style.

Figure out how to define limits for yourself

Defining limits for yourself assist you with turning out to be to a lesser degree an accommodating person. Saying OK and no to things that you do or don't have any desire to do. Assuming you say no, stick to it! Turning out to be excessively subject to others for joy or validation is significant not.

In the event that you are somebody who says 'OK' frequently when you begin to say no, it can and frequently makes issues since you are changing things and perceiving what's best for you. Over the long haul, saying no will become more straightforward and you will feel improved for getting it done.

Also, defining limits for you and supporting them in any event, during troublesome and testing times will assist you with turning out to be less mutually dependent. You would rather not become excessively subject to others for bliss or approval since then it becomes more enthusiasm for any other person to show up for you when things turn out badly (or even right).

The two accomplices should have their own lives beyond the relationship so they can be cheerful without having their necessities met by another person's satisfaction first. Doing this makes a reliant relationship, and assists you with defeating codependency.

Mutually dependent connections without limits become broken and challenging to make due. Sound limits are there which is as it should be.

Begin to rehearse care

Care is tied in with allowing yourself to feel what you feel. Its self-endorsement. You are sharing with yourself that you acknowledge how you feel and don't condemn yourself - anything your sentiments are.

I support these sentiments since it implies that I am traveling through something troublesome and I need to change. This is essential for my excursion. This is an incredible method for figuring out how to be available with yourself and with others without feeling like you want something from them constantly.

Care is the point at which you are aware of your viewpoints and sentiments, and you acknowledge them without condemning yourself or going down the supposed 'dark hole' rehashing a similar negative story you have been telling yourself.

Being more careful additionally about rehearsing contemplations.

On the off chance that you don't know how to begin with this training, have a go at contemplating for only five or ten minutes every day or basically seeing what's going on around you without passing judgment on it as sure or negative (this will assist with diminishing any nervousness).

Figure out how to make a reliant relationship

A reliant relationship includes and requires harmony between self and others inside the relationship. The two accomplices perceive that figuring out how to be available and meet each other's physical and close-to-home necessities in significant ways, is critical.

This incorporates every individual requiring some investment for their own advantages, having a solid sense of security and weak around each other, not depending on their accomplice to fulfill them, and having a sound identity regard. This sort of relationship is critical to making a protected, sound, and secure relationship and is the best kind of relationship.

Making and keeping a close-to-home association is vital to making a protected, sound, and secure relationship. The association that is worked between the two accomplices assists with making a more profound degree of grasping, seeing, hearing, and approving of each other. Furthermore, the strength of this association decides the outcome of a drawn-out relationship. This is a central component of a reliant relationship.

Work with psychological wellness proficient

Frequently a specialist can assist you with managing your codependency battles quicker than doing it all alone. They assist with uncovering the injury that frequently prompts these sorts of ways of behaving. For instance, an individual can become mutually dependent when they take on an unseemly profound obligation or they are 'parentified' (being put in a parental job very early on) to endure a horrible childhood. In treatment, this is talked about.

Perhaps your parent utilized you to discuss improper things (like cash) or relied upon you to meet their feelings.

In the event that this happened to you, you will start to disregard and neglect their requirements for your parent. Tragically, this turns into a learned way of behaving that from one viewpoint assists you with enduring your experience growing up however get you in a position to battle to keep up with sound connections as a grown-up.

Could a Mutually dependent Relationship at any point Be Fixed?

The short response - is yes. In spite of the fact that codependency is many times a difficult issue in connections, it tends to be fixed if both of you will roll out the improvements important to make your relationship work.

Mutually dependent individuals frequently feel like they have zero influence over their lives or their bliss, as they view their own joy as being subject to another person - however, this isn't correct. They need to figure out how to assume command over their life and their joy and perceive that every individual is answerable for their own life.

It's memorable's vital that the adoration you might feel for somebody you are mutually dependent on might be love, however, it might likewise be dread of being without them. The other bring-back home message is that there is significance in choosing to find ways to turn out to be less mutually dependent and figure out how to cherish yourself, put yourself first, and comprehend the qualities that contain a solid, reliant relationship.

The following are 4 things to recollect in managing codependency:

- Figure out how to find ways to figure out how to assume command over your life and joy and perceive that every individual is answerable for their own life.
- Mindfulness, making minuscule strides, sincerely promising to change - even a little one, and considering yourself responsible for these progressions are manners by which one, as well as the two individuals, can roll out the important improvements to

encounter self-awareness both independently and all in all as a couple.

- There is significance in choosing to find ways to turn out to be less mutually dependent and figure out how to cherish yourself, put yourself first, and comprehend the characteristics that contain a sound, reliant relationship.

- Getting some margin to roll out little improvements, after some time permits every individual to utilize their voice and offer what their requirements are in a solid manner, and this is finished through sure correspondence.

In any case, on the off chance that you have an undesirable mutually dependent relationship, reasonably, the individual you're with isn't great for your emotional wellness and prosperity.

The most effective way to turn out to be less mutually dependent in your relationship is to ensure that you're giving what's all for yourself and to acquire a superior and more profound comprehension of how you became mutually dependent.

Understanding this will permit you to 'unload' and change how you view yourself with regard to a relationship. Since recognizing how you became mutually dependent and the impacts of this on your relationship will help you turn and make another way for yourself as well as your relationship.

Furthermore, assuming you have a solid mutually dependent relationship, almost certainly, your accomplice draws out the best in you and assists you with developing personally. It can likewise be solid to figure out how to interface erring on a more profound level and become somewhat more 'needier'.

It very well may be trying to change your way of behaving, yet it is conceivable. Distinguishing how you became mutually dependent and the impacts of this on your relationship will help you turn and make another way for yourself as well as your relationship.

Yet, having mindfulness and comprehension of codependence can assist you with finding clearness and harmony in your connections and which can be the way to being less mutually dependent.

Change is generally conceivable.

CODEPENDENT FREE

CHAPTER EIGHT

Codependent Parents

Healing From Codependent Parents

At the point when we consider codependency in relationships or connections, we frequently partner the term mutually dependent with a harmful close connection. In all actuality, one of the most widely recognized types of codependency is mutually dependent guardians. Frequently accidentally, the child or little girl in the circumstance can empower the undesirable way of behaving of their parent. This can negatively affect kids and can cause enduring pessimistic consequences for the youngster's sentiments. To assist the parent, the two players with needing to comprehend codependency and how to recuperate from it.

What Is Codependency?

We frequently find out about codependency with regard to dependence. Research completed a couple of years prior characterizes codependency as "a mental condition or a relationship wherein an individual is controlled or controlled by one more who is impacted with a neurotic condition (like a dependence on liquor or heroin)." While partner codependency with enslavement is as yet normal, we see today that substance misuse isn't generally a component in mutually dependent individuals. Today, specialists and clinicians have a superior comprehension of codependency and realize individuals can become dependent on an individual, and online treatment has been demonstrated to be an incredible asset while exploring codependency.

Codependency is some of the time alluded to as a "relationship fixation" since somebody can turn out to be so reliant upon someone else to the mark of enslavement. This dependence could in fact take structure in a parent-kid relationship. Guardians can turn out to be sincerely and intellectually dependent on their youngsters while managing what is going on. A mutually dependent parent will depend on their youngster for their wellspring of bliss, mental security, and confidence. At the point when the parent loses a feeling of control, they can attack their kids, and can at times have serious breakdowns. The youngster being relied upon can encounter an extremely profound cost as the mutually dependent parent's joy is in their grasp.

The Impacts Of Codependency

Associations with mutually dependent individuals can frequently be genuinely oppressive and disastrous. At the point when a kid has mutually dependent guardians, they can encounter an enduring pessimistic effect on their psychological well-being, the capacity to understand individuals on a profound level, and future connections. Tragically, studies or insights about youngsters who experience the wake of growing up with a mutually dependent parent are deficient. In any case, specialists truly do realize the issue is turning out to be increasingly more common every year.

Guardians and watchmen assume a major part in assisting a youngster with growing genuinely and intellectually. The point when a kid has mutually dependent guardians, shapes their future qualities and conduct. Kids get on their folks' ways of behaving and impersonate them. Codependency can be one of the numerous ways of behaving gained from a parent. Like different types of dependence, codependency can include family, so it is vital to be cautious while bringing an opportunity for a youngster of creating it.

Research by the College School Arizona shows that youngsters with less control, however, additional caring guardians were bound to be more joyful and more fulfilled in their grown-up years. We realize that an individual battling with codependency feels as though they need to have command over their kid or, in all likelihood they experience tension or stress.

Guardians will apply some degree of command over their youngsters, however, mutually dependent guardians will take control of something else altogether. When both a mutually dependent mother and mutually dependent dad apply overabundance command over a kid and are excessively involved, studies recommend this can diminish life fulfillment and hurt the psychological prosperity of the small kid or grown-up youngster.

A mutually dependent parent making their youngster liable for their own adult struggles can truly hurt a kid's character, possibly causing low confidence and the absence of identity viability. A mutually dependent parent might try and make their youngster feel remorseful as they battle with getting a sense of ownership with things that are not age-fitting for the kid's life. To this end, it is so vital to treat codependency issues whenever they are analyzed.

Indications Of A Mutually dependent Parent

Very much like with some other fixation, codependency appears to be unique for everybody. It is essential to shun self-diagnosing, and on second thought look for a conclusion from an authorized instructor or a clinician. Yet, for an indication of mutually dependent parent codependency, read the rundown of certain signs that there is codependency in a parent-kid relationship:

- Undesirable mental control of the youngster's life through manipulation or psychological mistreatment

- State of mind swings or outrage issues in the event that there is ever an absence of control
- Excessively profound way of behaving during a contention, as they quickly shift starting with one state of mind and then onto the next
- Trouble having discussions without lashing out or rankled
- Will in general have a casualty mindset regardless of whether they were some unacceptable one
- Conveying intimidation to persuade the other to do what they need
- Mistaking pity for compassion
- Being detached and forceful when they don't get things their way
- Involving quiet treatment in a bid to acquire control and compliance

There could be numerous alternate ways codependency shows itself in connections. The regular method for knowing whether somebody has codependency issues is to get analyzed by an authorized proficient.

Might A Parent-Kid Relationship at any point Return To Ordinary After Codependency?

With the right limits and care, a parent-kid relationship can be solid again after codependency. Typically, the restorative way of behaving needs in the first place the parent, particularly in the event that the kid is early in life. There are a few stages that have been distinguished by experts for getting making progress toward a sound parent-youngster relationship.

Moves toward Recuperate a Relationship

Connections that have experienced a type of compulsion should be treated with cherishing care. While attempting to stop the cynicism that codependency brings, it is vital to be cautious, aware, and delicate consistently. It very well might be troublesome, yet intently following these means might possibly fix a harmed relationship.

- Look for the assistance of an accomplished expert with codependency or compulsion. Directing meetings with authorized treatment will probably prompt improved results.

- Have open correspondence while remaining cool-headed and conscious of each other. This is a cycle that should break to accomplish predictability once more.

Mistaken About Managing For Mutually dependent Guardians (And How To Recuperate)?

Give youngsters more opportunity and command over themselves and their own characters. In certain circumstances, years will go by with the youngster feeling as though they have zero power over their choices in view of the mutually dependent examples of a parent, even as they go into grown-up business and life in "this present reality." As referenced over, a kid should have a feeling of freedom for them to construct fearlessness and have a more noteworthy possibility of feeling happy with their healthy identity and future.

To quit being mutually dependent, put down stopping points in mutually dependent connections. Defining limits, assumptions, and rules with a mutually dependent parent is a major piece of having a sound parent-kid relationship. With mutually dependent guardians, almost certainly, limits have never been set. It is ideal to define limits, so there are clear principles in the relationship pushing ahead.

Be excusing when limits are crossed, and when rules are broken. Recuperating from a mutually dependent parent-youngster relationship is a long excursion for the two players, and it will be intense. Pardoning ought to be openly given when one party is really upset about their way of behaving. The kid ought to recollect their parent is managing an analyzed condition that causes their way of behaving. It ought to be noticed that mutually dependent guardians can utilize control to control youngsters, and intentionally crossing limits isn't OK.

Step by step instructions to Mend Subsequent to Growing Up With Mutually dependent Guardians

Growing up with mutually dependent guardians as a youngster is unquestionably hard, and extends into a grown-up kid's life. The negative and controlling way of behaving of a mutually dependent parent is displayed to lastingly affect the youngster who is subject to them. When kid arrives at adulthood, having sound fellowships and heartfelt connections can challenge them. This grown-up kid may likewise apply the learned mutually dependent ways of behaving of undesirable connection in their future family or with their own youngsters too. Be that as it may, daily reassurance and sound limits are feasible for the two youngsters and grown-up kids who have managed a mutually dependent parent.

Guiding

To try not to experience the ill effects of codependency later on, specialists suggest grown-up kids and parents in this present circumstance look for help from an authorized guide to manage their sentiments and own necessities. This can assist with breaking the generational impact a mutually dependent relationship has on kids and guardians, and train an individual to define sound limits.

In the event that the "kid" is presently a grown-up, they ought to consider going to relationship advising with their accomplice. We figure out how to treat others, including our children, from our folks, and growing up with mutually dependent guardians is certainly not an optimal climate to learn in. Regardless of whether the grown-up kid isn't seeing someone their heartfelt connection is sound, and guiding can furnish individuals with everyday reassurance and solid relationship abilities, they had not mastered previously.

Done Empowering

In an ideal world, the relationship will be fixed and can be sound in the future. This would be perfect and would assist with reducing the hurtful impacts of codependency. As a general rule, this doesn't necessarily occur. Very much like with different types of compulsion, the individual battling may not want to recuperate or gain little headway. In this situation, youngsters must quit empowering their way of behaving.

Done empowering destructive way of behaving can be different for every relationship. One of the simplest ways is to say, "You are breaking my limits, and I won't be controlled." This removes the parent from their, strategic, influential place and can assist them with acknowledging what they are doing over and again. Frequently, the empowering agent feels in charge in the event that they can start feeling in their youngster. Attempting to not respond to the parent's horrendous acts and words is likewise an extraordinary move toward at this point not empower.

Managing Mutually dependent Guardians

Getting a mutually dependent parent's assistance is a caring and bold step for any youngster to make, regardless of what age they are. Being relied upon for another person's bliss is a lot of liability that no individual could be ready for. The most effective way to help is to get the mutually dependent parent the assistance they with requiring from an authorized specialist so they can stop their way of behaving. It is additionally enthusiastically suggested the youngster in the circumstance looks for advice to assist them with feeling sure about having great connections later on.

CHAPTER NINE

Codependency Exercise

This chapter will assist us with understanding the idea of codependency and what it means for our life unfavorably. Yet, more critically, it gives us the solution to the inquiry "What are the activities used to manage codependency?" and a lot of additional intriguing viewpoints about codependency.

How is codependency works out?

To assist manage codependency a few activities lessen the effect of codependency and give help from its unfortunate results.

- Rehearsing Taking care of oneself and Development
- Further developing Critical thinking abilities
- Zeroing in on becoming Autonomous
- Managing horrendous past

There are different side effects of codependency yet one of its center side effects could be considered as a limit and unfortunate reliance on an individual, some of the time even a substance or interaction (the cycle could be a movement like betting or even sexual exercises). At the point when we are in charge of this condition we lose our concentration and confidence in ourselves and begin focusing on some other person or thing more than ourselves. Our life begins rotating around that other thing rather than ourselves which further decays our condition. To beat this incapacitating state and reconnect with ourselves we really want to observe specific rules and rules. The following are sure useful changes we could make in our lives to conquer codependency.

Forbearance.

Rehearsing forbearance or restraint is imperative to conquer codependency. This aids in moving the concentration and consideration from others back to yourself. By doing this move you convey the message that your life is represented by your needs, needs, and values rather than other people. While the facts really confirm that complete restraint is an unthinkable undertaking as you truly do require some sort of reliance on others to make due throughout everyday life. Be that as it may, the objective here is to have a solid degree of reliance and, surprisingly, a specific degree of separation. This separation guarantees that you don't fixate, on control, control, or invest your energy in satisfying others. All things considered, you become an independent and free individual.

Mindfulness

It is fundamental to know about one's concerns to manage them. Frequently mutually dependent people are trying to claim ignorance of their concerns and push the fault onto others. They are likewise trying to claim ignorance of their own sentiments and beliefs that cause them should carry on with an exceptionally frustrating life.

Frequently an individual's young life experience adds to the improvement of such muddled sentiments and contemplations, In the event that our feelings weren't met or on the other hand on the off chance that we weren't brought up in a sincerely sustaining climate in our experience growing up we foster a distorted idea of closeness. After some time as opposed to yearning for affection that was never given we will more often than not focus on others over us as we begin viewing ourselves as useless or undeserving. We could likewise foster a few unfortunate and horrendous propensities, for example, substance misuse, dietary problems, compulsive fixation on sex, and so on. Hence to try not to go down this way it is vital to know about our condition, needs, and needs and to recognize them suitably.

Acknowledgment

Another significant step includes unqualified self-acknowledgment. Commonly we are not content with what our identity is or what we have become and dismiss ourselves. Be that as it may, acknowledgment is a vital part of recuperating and recuperation.

It is additionally a sign that you have chosen to embrace yourself with every one of your imperfections and not stress over others' perspectives or considerations. It shows the world that you are not generally shackled by others' needs and needs and will just care for your own prosperity from here onwards. Self-acknowledgment helps in reestablishing your confidence and furthermore achieves numerous positive and sound changes inside you. You become more grounded and more decisive. Rather than being manipulative and fanatical, you figure out how to become normal and bona fide.

Action

While it is important to have mindfulness and be OK you likewise need to make a reasonable move to advance your thighs further. This activity is only better than ever conduct as the result of the multitude of past changes done by the person. It additionally includes getting out of your usual range of familiarity and standing up to your apprehensions. It is important to evaluate new things or take part in exercises you won't ever investigate. These new encounters will open new roads for you and make you a new, improved, and better person. It likewise comprises laying out limits so you can have a good sense of reassurance and make a sound. Confidence is a quality that gives us the capacity o come to a meaningful conclusion and carry on with our existence certainly. It additionally helps in fostering our certainty and confidence consequently we want to concentrate and act toward creating decisiveness. Since just when we figure out how to stand up for ourselves will individuals pay attention to us and regard our contemplations, sentiments, and thoughts.

Practices for codependency

Rehearsing Taking care of oneself and Development

We catch wind of rehearsing and taking care of ourselves consistently and think that it is dreary and tedious and don't really think about it. However, we don't understand the potential acquires that we could get from dealing with ourselves. Somebody with mutually dependent propensities frequently focuses on others' requirements over their own making it hard for them to deal with themselves.

They frequently penance their own needs and needs and end up hopeless. It is essential to comprehend for such people are entirely alone and doesn't others to track down the importance of their life. Taking care of oneself gives sustenance and empowers the development and advancement of a person. It likewise clears a path for freedom and strengthening which are fundamental variables in an individual's life. We can rehearse taking care of ourselves by doing contemplation, participating in exercises that give delight and satisfaction to us, or in any event, making a new and better schedule that can be viewed as taking care of oneself.

Further developing Critical thinking abilities

It has been seen that mutually dependent people experience difficulty pursuing choices for their life. They are convinced, hopefully not by mistake, that they aren't fit to deal with this obligation and could wind up accomplishing something wrong. This winds up influencing their certainty level and confidence. However, this mainly exacerbates the situation for themselves and further expands their reliance on others. To dispose of this conduct at whatever point what is going on emerges when you need to pursue a choice attempt to ask yourself, "What will be the most ideal decision for me in this present circumstance given my ongoing conditions?". They're going to be times when you'll bad decisions, but when this happens you should try to accept the situation as it is. In any case, that is only a piece of the example and gradually you will wind up with better critical thinking abilities.

Zeroing in on Autonomy

Freedom is practically similar to an unfamiliar word for individuals used to codependency. In any case, it is exceptionally fundamental to develop free conduct to dispose of codependency. The individual doesn't have to start practicing freedom without skipping a beat in terrific ways and signals. They can begin with little moves to assist them with getting adjusted to the circumstance. It very well may be heading out to the films alone or in any event, eating at an eatery. You could likewise go for a walk in the recreation area or visit puts that you generally wished to see. You could do everything that you recently did with someone so you wouldn't feel alone or awkward. This exercise means to assist you with the understanding that being distant from everyone else with your own contemplations doesn't is definitely not an upsetting encounter and we can appreciate things all alone also without taking any other individual's help.

Managing Past Injury

Previous encounters that are horrendous in nature can frequently be a reason for the improvement of codependency. Consequently, it is important to promptly look for help for these issues. These issues could assume a part in influencing your confidence as well as certainty which thus adversely influences your codependency side effects. Hence the sooner we settle these issues the less they would influence our psychological wellness. The best solution for such issues is to look for treatment. Treatment is truly outstanding and the most sought-after treatment technique to manage mental and profound injury. It furnishes you with the essential devices to battle a wide range of issues emerging because of your horrible past. Treatment doesn't simply assist you with managing your previous issues yet in addition the ongoing issues emerging because of codependency. It could give arrangements and methods to assist manage the negative parts of codependency in connections and assist you with accomplishing a sound and satisfying relationship.

CODEPENDENT FREE

CHAPTER TEN

Diary Prompts for Healing Codependency

In spite of the fact that codependency recuperation requires some investment, composing prompts are an extraordinary method for bouncing beginning the cycle. Diary prompts incorporate composed activities to assist you with looking at old ways of behaving and recuperating them.

Albeit many individuals look for treatment or potentially go to 12-step gatherings (which I profoundly empower), these composing activities will assist you with beginning the way of recuperation.

Codependency Recuperation

Codependency recuperation is the method involved with forgetting broken designs and making self-trust and commonly fulfilling connections. Building confidence without depending on outside approval is an essential objective. Recuperation work implies figuring out how to esteem yourself and what you really want.

These diary prompts will recognize significant regions in the recuperation cycle. Recall little yet consistently comes out on top in the race!

7 Diary Prompts for Mending Codependency

1. How might you zero in additional on yourself?

Mutually dependent individuals frequently disregard themselves for other people. In spite of the fact that they love being the legend, zeroing in a lot on others causes them to feel restless, overpowered, and discouraged. Some foster pressure-related sicknesses.

All things being equal, consider what you really want to care more for yourself. Begin by surveying your actual requirements for good food, rest, workout, and so on. Taking care of these basic yet frequently overlooked regions will assist you with feeling more grounded.

Second, are there interests and leisure activities that have been ignored on the grounds that your energy went to helping other people?

On the off chance that indeed, consider what means a lot to you. Might you at any point allow yourself to invest a portion of your effort towards what you need rather than continuously falling once more into what others need?

Task: Make a rundown of taking care of oneself exercises that would make life more charming. What region of your own life could you at any point begin zeroing in on?

2. What limits do you have to begin setting?

Mutually dependent individuals lose all sense of direction in others' concerns. Others' aggravation and experiencing will quite often overwhelm the mutually dependent individual's reasoning. They need so seriously to help yet lose themselves all the while.

In recuperation, the objective is to track down a harmony between focusing on taking care of oneself and providing for other people. Changing this example can move connections from being uneven to being valuable together.

To start, recognize one region where you feel overpowered and consider what limits could help.

For example:

Is there a circumstance where you're fed up with making a difference?

Might you at any point give less in one aspect of your life?

Might you at some point remain quiet as opposed to chipping in?

Could you at any point plan some time consistently for taking care of yourself?

Task: Pick one region where you will say no or shout out about what will work for you.

3. How might you start to withdraw from unfortunate circumstances?

Mutually dependent individuals feel overpowered and undervalued in their connections. They will generally draw in individuals who are dependent or have heaps of issues that need fixing.

The good-natured mutually dependent attempts to fix what is happening by applying control. This triggers the other individual to move cautiously and pull away. Nobody likes being determined about what to do and despite the fact that they have good intentions, mutually dependent individuals wind up making more turmoil.

Attempting to help somebody that would rather not be helped is depleting! All things considered, working on adoring separation can save your mental soundness. Separation implies relinquishing control to the point of taking the concentration back to your own life.

Task: How is it that you could start to withdraw so you can return to your own life?

4. How might you quit stressing over others' opinions of you?

Mutually dependent individuals fanatically stress over others' thought processes of them. Their confidence comes from outer approval so facing this issue is quite difficult. Rehearsing tenderness towards self here is significant. Cherishing oneself takes time and readiness to track down the positive qualities in ourselves.

Once more, the course of recuperation implies not getting into others' heads (which is where the mutually dependent stalls out) but rather zeroing in on oneself.

For example, could you at any point praise yourself for a wonderful piece of handiwork or headway made as opposed to seeking others for affirmation? On the off chance that you commit an error, could you at any point be delicate with yourself like you could do with a companion?

Task: When you notice yourself agonizing over the thing others are thinking, get your emphasis back on something you want to accomplish for your own recuperation.

5. How might you relinquish attempting to be awesome and try not to commit errors?

Having unreasonable assumptions for yourself is really difficult for mutually dependent people. Feeling that they ought to constantly be the best is the means by which they characterize themselves.

Sadly, this makes a great deal of inward pressure that makes nervousness a deep-rooted battle. Committing errors becomes unsatisfactory, so they try not to attempt new things.

All things considered, the objective is to embrace their flaws and practice self-acknowledgment. In the event that they're bringing up youngsters, halting the pattern of flawlessness can be a spurring factor. Most mutually dependent individuals grow up accepting that they must be ideal to be adored. Passing that conviction onto their kids can be a reminder.

Task: Endeavor to embrace areas of flaw. Everybody has little idiosyncrasies that should be visible as charming to those they love. Where can "being flawed" reduce your heap?

6. Where might you at any point request help or backing?

Mutually dependent individuals highly esteem thoroughly taking care of every other person while never requesting help. Obviously, this makes life harder than it should be. Individual issues are dealt with in detachment as they would rather not trouble anybody or bring about any possible surprise.

Fears of being viewed as self-centered or feeble are normal with issues of codependency. Since their young life encounters weren't approved, the mutually dependent individual grows up with a pile of self-question. They have no faith in that assistance will with being offered, so they don't inquire.

Doing life alone feels more secure than the gamble of being powerless, however, they are unimaginably desolate accordingly.

Task: Who in your life might want to help you here and there? Consider going to treatment or computer-based intelligence Anon assuming that you really want more direction.

7. How might you start to trust your own discernments and sentiments?

Mutually dependent individuals seek others for approval as opposed to confiding as far as they can tell. They take extraordinary measures to satisfy others as opposed to confiding in their own faculties and instinct.

Believing yourself begins by regarding your own insight - without judgment or analysis. Perhaps it's a premonition or an internal knowing that advises you to give close consideration. While instinct might appear to be unique for every individual, we as a whole have it in some structure.

Task: Work on getting to understand what your own instinct resembles and begin involving it for direction. This will incredibly improve with time.

CODEPENDENT FREE

CHAPTER ELEVEN

Limits and the Dance of the Codependent

Adore and Esteem Yourself In Your Relationship With Others

An extremely well-known point in codependency writing is the test that a mutually dependent has in defining sound limits.

We should investigate codependency, from an outline of the regular ways of behaving and the reasons for those ways of behaving. Codependency is definitely not an emotional well-being conclusion; rather, it is an educated way of behaving, frequently created in youth. The vast majority of mutually dependent people, come from useless families, frequently with a background marked by codependency and dependent, self-involved, or depressed accomplices.

The mutually dependent parent and the junkie or egomaniac sets the example for how youngsters see a relationship. Youngsters gain from the mutually dependent parent to put in more effort in the relationship, to give all to fulfill the requirements of the egotist, dependent, or even harmful parent, and that in some way they can roll out the improvements expected to address or fix the relationship.

It is entirely expected in these kinds of broken families for youngsters to really take on a parental job as the guardians are too up to speed in the elements of their own disastrous relationship. Youngsters figure out how to "tread lightly," how to keep their necessities stowed away and put the requirements of others prior to all the other things, and how the presentation of the relationship is of the most extreme significance.

Youngsters who get familiar with these illustrations and don't figure out how to encourage their own self-esteem and worth, and to consider themselves to be a significant and independent individual, battle with future connections. They are continuously searching for somebody to fix,

fix, or take care of, instead of finding an accomplice who is secure, free, and cherishing.

In the event that this sounds recognizable, and really focusing on the requirements of your accomplice is a higher priority than being blissful yourself, you might be mutually dependent. You might have a lot of trouble in defining limits in the relationship, and you might track down that even the possibility of saying "no" to the accomplice might cause nervousness if they somehow managed to end up being irate, disappointed, or upset.

Simultaneously, you feel troubled in the relationship. Most mutually dependent people feel caught in a relationship, however, they should be with somebody as opposed to all alone is a seriously startling idea simultaneously, exceptionally normal for an individual who is mutually dependent to feel baffled and, surprisingly, furious at how much energy and time they spend in a relationship with next to no response. After some time, this annoyance and dissatisfaction fabricate, however, it is normally turned inwards as communicating outrage and disdain to the accomplice just builds the gamble of contention and antagonism, the very things the mutually dependent needs to keep away from in the battle to make the "great" relationship.

The opposite side of the coin can likewise happen with a mutually dependent. After some time, the dissatisfaction with the steady requests and depletes on significant investment develops and brings about suddenly erupts against the accomplice. It might likewise result in the mutually dependent picking an accomplice that needs a guardian, permitting the mutually dependent to have some degree of control. Simultaneously, the broken accomplice is impervious to this control and is likewise suddenly erupting, making struggle and an absence of control all through the relationship.

The basis of the entirety of this contention and struggle, both inside and inside the relationship, is in many cases brought about by an absence of limits. The mutually dependent will think twice about their own satisfaction and necessities to endeavor to make a positive relationship with a never be fulfilled. individual.

At some level, the mutually dependent perceives this disparity but on the other hand, is unfortunate of being dismissed and has a feeling of dread toward a showdown. Keep in mind, the objective of the mutually dependent is to make everything fit their concept of the ideal couple and how that ought to appear to everyone around them. Saying "no" or deciding to do something of significance to them instead of to the accomplice is contradictory to accomplishing this objective.

What Are Limits?

Limits are the standards or the undetectable walls or fences that gap individuals and keep the physical, close-to-home, and mental components of life separate from those of the others around you.

Limits are additionally the guidelines by which we let individuals in on what we will acknowledge and what we don't acknowledge. At the point when we neglect to define limits for ourselves, we naturally and of course permit others to define those limits. We likewise free ourselves up to managing silly and nonsensical assumptions by those able to take too much.

All in all, how would you define limits, and how do others have any idea about what those limits are?

The way to define limits is to tell others they exist. As a speedy model, envision you had a kid and permitted her to get to anything she needed to eat in the kitchen, and you gave no dietary limits. Kids normally pick food sources that they like and would enjoy frozen yogurt, treats, chips, and different sorts of food sources, ordinarily staying away from quality food varieties like vegetables and natural products.

Guardians normally put down stopping points with kids about food and let them in on the guidelines and assumptions. This might incorporate having a little serving of frozen yogurt subsequent to completing your feast or having treats periodically and in restricted numbers.

Kids become familiar with these limits when the standard is made sense of. That doesn't mean they won't test those limits, and the parent must be firm and predictable. Through articulating the limit and afterward being predictable, a standard is made that considers the positive parts of the way of behaving yet additionally gives care and insurance.

Similar kinds of limits are required to see someone. In any case, as we have recently taken a gander at mutually dependent ways of behaving, it is not difficult to see the reason why setting these relationship rules or fences and holding to them will be a test.

Mutually dependent people might comprehend the limits they need, however upholding them turns into an issue. To make matters significantly more troublesome, the egotistical or dependent accomplice is really quite mindful of the dynamic and enjoys incredible pushing and controlling these limits or driving directly through them.

The normal reasons that limits are difficult for mutually dependent people include:

- Apprehension about conflict - just the demonstration of facing the accomplice might be overpowering for the mutually dependent, especially assuming that these sorts of issues have brought about the accomplice leaving, taking steps to leave, or turning out to be sincerely or truly oppressive previously.

- Absence of comprehension of necessities - on the off chance that you never know limits in connections, remembering for your associations with guardians, it is hard to tell what you want.
- The conviction others are more significant - the profoundly imbued conviction that the other individual is more significant and necessary to start things out is a mind-boggling factor in the test of building limits and keeping up with them.
- Apprehension about the loss of endorsement - when the accomplice has consistently had his direction in the relationship, especially with an egotist, defining limits will prompt an absence of endorsement. For the mutually dependent, this is the greatest trepidation, and working with a specialist or holistic mentor during this time is instrumental to creating viable survival techniques and not simply only surrendering and returning to the old absence of limits relationship.

- Assuming the fault course - some mutually dependent people become irritating or forceful when they attempt to define limits. Rather than defining the limit and finishing, they continually rehash data, scrutinize or fault the other individual for the adjustment of the relationship "controls." This might prompt the mutually dependent to take steps to leave or to accomplish something she won't do, which supports the absence of limits when the accomplice challenges this new need or worth.
- Absence of help - it is likewise normal for an individual in a mutually dependent relationship to be genuinely and socially disconnected. All things considered, your time is spent attempting to satisfy your accomplice, and loved ones are frequently disregarded or gotten over. This seclusion and absence of help benefit the egotist, fiend, or sincerely harmful accomplice as he knows he is your main association.
- Low confidence and self-esteem - in the event that you are mutually dependent, you have a low identity worth and confidence.

This makes it hard to see yourself as deserving of the admiration of others, which makes it a test to have the option to define these limits and afterward finish results in the event that they are followed.

Fortunately, these kinds of convictions, fears, and issues can be changed. It's vital to learn better approaches for defining limits that are engaging, give taking care of oneself, and assist you with having a decent outlook on yourself and the people around you.

Moving beyond These Limit Boundaries

Moving beyond limits and setting fears and boundaries is difficult. It requires investment, support, and an eagerness to figure out how to trust in your worth of yourself. It is feasible to figure out how to draw well-spoken lines in any relationship, and afterward likewise set results you will use to consider yourself responsible for those limits.

The keys to defining limits include:

- Cherishing yourself - the initial step is to start the excursion of figuring out how to cherish yourself and foster an identity worth and self-esteem. It is an educational experience, and it includes forgetting that large number of negative messages and being available to check out yourself according to a totally new perspective.

- Understanding what you esteem - limits are general; they are not all-inclusive for all individuals. What one individual might acknowledge in a relationship, another may not. In any case, what is acknowledged must be solid, positive, and helpful, or it's anything but a powerful limit inside the relationship. Investigating what you are worth and what you really want is the beginning stage for defining limits that are important and significant.

- Investigate what you believe you should do - frequently time and needs are an issue for mutually dependent people. They fear losing their fellowship or status, so they say "OK" to everything, in any event, when they don't have the opportunity or the energy to do the things they have resolved to finish. By figuring out how to carve out an opportunity to consider what you believe should do and focusing on your time, it is simpler to track down ways of saying "no" or "I'm occupied around then," without feeling overpowered with responsibility and dread or loathing yourself for not defending your necessities.

- Discuss limits - conversing with advocates, mentors, companions, and relatives can be exceptionally astute in understanding how they put down stopping points. Understanding how limits are utilized in a wide range of connections and not simply in cozy accomplice connections can be both instructive as well as educational.

- Work on imparting messages - figuring out how to explain and convey your necessities, needs, and values is generally fundamental. This might seem like learning another dialect, especially on the off chance that you are an individual who has never spoken about her necessities. Rehearsing how to convey is a central expertise to dominate in your connections.

It is additionally crucial for connecting for help. Figuring out how to define limits and holding yourself to those limits without yielding or returning to old, unfortunate ways of behaving is confounded and hard. There will be times when it appears to be more straightforward just to surrender, however every time you give in you send yourself, and the other individual a message. That message is that you are not of worth in the relationship, which is unquestionably not the situation.

Over the long run, defining and keeping up with limits turns out to be more agreeable. There might be times you begin to think adversely, just need to keep away from the showdown, or are sincerely drained, yet even in these circumstances, you can have serious areas of strength to be, emphatic, and work on focusing on yourself.

CODEPENDENT FREE

CHAPTER TWELVE

Helping a Companion In a Mutually Dependent Relationship

At some point back, I had a companion in a mutually dependent relationship. How could I know this? I was continuously conversing with her on the telephone as she called me endlessly time again to discuss a few issues in her relationship. However much every relationship has its difficulties, a mutually dependent relationship can deplete.

How could I realize my companion is in a mutually dependent relationship?

From a portion of the issues she could discuss, I pieced an endless flow of pieces and understood quite that, that was a mutually dependent relationship. A portion of those signs are;

Continually making splits the difference for the other individual

She was continually making penances for the other individual, regardless of whether these trade-offs made her miserable. It was consistently split the difference in succession. All she appeared to do is offer and get nothing as a trade-off. For any individual, this can feel depleting, and feeling overlooked can genuinely pressure you.

Making their accomplice aggravate their own

You can have compassion for your accomplice when they are going through a difficult stretch, however, be mindful so as not to incorporate their agony. At the point when you love them, it is difficult to see them enduring, and you identify with their aggravation and solace them. In any case, when you make their aggravation your own, this can be undesirable.

It isn't your job to protect your accomplice from their aggravation and on the off chance that it feels this, this is unfortunate. You can uphold your accomplice and assist them with getting themselves away from their test get you ought to foster a limit to keep you free.

Treading lightly

In the event that you continually feel disgrace, tension, feeling of dread toward committing errors, anxiety toward being judged, or on the other hand in the event that you accomplish something wrong your accomplice will leave, these are indications of a mutually dependent relationship. A solid relationship ought to be one in which you are blissful and you really want not to tread lightly for the anxiety toward culpable your accomplice.

Assuming your relationship gives you tension and dread and you are continually terrified of accomplishing something that will insult your accomplice, then this relationship isn't solid in any way. Different signs are, for example, hatred and outrage that you might feel are achieved by your accomplice.

They continually safeguard their accomplice

Obviously, in any great relationship, you ought to be in your accomplice's corner. Be that as it may, in a few unfortunate connections, you hear every one of the horrible things your companion's accomplice does to them, but they actually safeguard this individual. Forswearing is one of the early indications of a mutually dependent relationship. In the event that you bring up something their accomplice isn't doing well, they rush to bring up that their accomplice is a decent individual and has only good intentions.

You feel that your accomplice controls everything

In the event that your companion enlightens you regarding their accomplice pursuing every one of the choices and maybe your companion has nothing to do with their relationship, this is undesirable. Mutually dependent individuals like to take control since it causes them to have a good sense of reassurance and security in a relationship. In a solid relationship, people are dynamic members of navigation.

The most effective method to help a companion in a mutually dependent relationship

Assist them with perceiving that they are in a mutually dependent relationship

An individual can't tackle being in a mutually dependent relationship in the event that they don't realize that they are in a mutually dependent relationship. The initial step to aiding them is by causing them to understand that they are in a mutually dependent relationship.

You can do this by featuring things in their relationship that might appear to be typical to the couple yet they shout warnings and codependency contrasted with ordinary connections. I likewise have expounded on signs you are in a mutually dependent relationship which you can use to assist them with investigating how mutually dependent their relationship is.

Assist them with creating mindfulness

Assist your companion with becoming mindful and thusly work on their certainty and regard. Mindfulness will assist your companion with finding out more about herself, her assets, and her weaknesses. Mindfulness prompts self-understanding and self-acknowledgment.

At the point when you are mindful, you don't have to feel approved by others. You are sure of what your identity is, blemishes and all, and subsequently less inclined to create mutually dependent ways of behaving. Similarly, when you are mindful, you are less inclined to want to support someone else's mutually dependent way of behaving. You figure out how to make sound limits and along these lines

Help them reparent themselves

We frequently create mutually dependent propensities or support mutually dependent connections since we have not recuperated from our young life wounds. Ways of behaving, for example, continuously attempting to satisfy others and over-compromising root in youth issues like surrender and disregard by guardians.

Be strong

At times individuals in such connections can find it hard to stop particularly in the event that there are kids required, among different entanglements. You can help a companion in a mutually dependent relationship by being strong, standing by listening to them as they vent, and just being their companion. At the point when you support them, they realize they are cherished and will with time foster the certainty to attract limits their relationship.

Assist them with leaving

In some cases, mutually dependent connections can be tackled through treatment, correspondence, and readiness to cooperate. Nonetheless, in the event that one accomplice isn't willing to deal with the relationship, you can help a companion by empowering them to leave the relationship. Codependency is never sound and is probably going to deteriorate with time.

Frequently, individuals are reluctant to leave their connections since they feel as though they have put such a great amount into the relationship and this sounds like surrendering. Certain individuals need an additional push to leave awful circumstances. You can assist a companion with portraying how cheerful they would be without their accomplice in a lot more joyful and solid relationship. This can assist them with acknowledging they merit better and leave a mutually dependent relationship.

Decisively, helping a companion in a mutually dependent relationship isn't simple, particularly on the off chance that they see nothing amiss with their relationship. It might take determinedly conversing with them over the long run, being strong, and assisting them with gradually acknowledging how unfortunate the relationship is. In the event that you don't figure out how to save them from a terrible relationship, recollect that you were an old buddy and attempted to help.

CHAPTER THIRTEEN

Healing a Codependent Friendship

You can be mutually dependent on connections other than heartfelt ones. It is normal for people with mutually dependent reasoning propensities to carry those equivalent propensities to our fellowships. What do you do on the off chance that a companion doesn't give however much you do assuming you feel made the most of in kinship in the event that a companion doesn't text or call however much you do in the event that a companion rests on you for a ton of exhortation in any event, when you're truly going through it?

We should begin by discussing limits. As mutually dependent and human-satisfying masterminds, we are much of the time tested by the idea of limits. Frequently in light of the fact that we didn't grow up with sound limits or cutoff points demonstrated for us by our adults. Or on the other hand, we discovered that to be a great young lady, to be adorable (in light of the man-centric society). We need to give more than we truly need to keep others cheerful.

The center injury of mutually dependent reasoning is accepting that we must be everything to everybody, other than ourselves obviously.

At the point when you pair that with obtaining our value remotely, it's a good idea that we believe it's our work in life to oversee others' lives and temperaments them. To be a constant teacher's pet. Frustrating somebody by talking about our reality and saying no is only unbelievable from the beginning.

Limits are fundamental to blissful, solid, commonly steady associated connections, which is the objective of defeating codependency. In codependency, we don't have any idea where we end and another person starts. Limits are a method for isolating that out. At the point when we don't talk about our cutoff points or put them down and continue to stop points — "assuming you X, I will do Y" — we can get enmeshed with individuals in our lives. We can end their life as our concern, as our own to oversee when that is simply not the situation. From that enmeshment, we lose our singular character and take on the preferences, inclinations, sentiments, and feelings of the other individual like they were our own.

In mutually dependent reasoning, we have lost our anchor inside ourselves. We don't have faith in our own values since we exist. We have lost our association with our realness. All things considered, we chameleon, shape-moving to be, say, and do what we think others maintain that we should be, say and do.

At the point when you're enmeshed with another person, a companion, accomplice, work, kid, or parent, you develop the obligations of codependency there.

You forget about what your identity is and who you need to be on the planet increasingly more every day.

When you don't have any idea what YOU really need, how might you deal with yourself? How might you take care of yourself? How might you parse out what your own requirements and needs are?

As human vertebrates, we really want each other. Association, fellowship, and co-guideline of our sensory system is an essential pieces of being a pack creature, which we are. Being associated with different people, with companions who truly have our backs is crucial to our well-being. The issue is one of degrees and energetics - the contemplations and sentiments you bring to the association.

There is a colossal distinction between "I figure it would be good to work this choice out with my BFF" and "omg, I can't settle on this choice without her feedback!"

What I'm highlighting here is the Buddhist idea of getting a handle on, which is a type of experience that comes sticking to a person or thing for our profound well-being. This getting a handle on prompts superfluous enduring when we make one individual our beginning and end, rather than making OURSELVES and our own viewpoint needs and needs our actual north star.

At the point when there is no personal distance, no separation, and hazy limits it's so natural to slip into making another person, a companion, or a sweetheart, your outright everything. This can prompt difficult uneven characters in power elements, which is likewise a vital part of mutually dependent reasoning.

So when one individual is the provider and one is the taker in manners that are lopsided, we become dependent on that lively trade and forget about our own personalities.

We can get excessively dependent on our companions to fill an excruciating opening in our souls. We come to rely upon them to approve our decisions, and to allow us to would what we like to do. We go to our BFF to let us know that we are OK, sufficient, and deserving of adoration in a traditionally mutually dependent manner that removes us from living in our own power and obtaining our value inside.

So what are the indications of companionship all disturbed up in mutually dependent reasoning?

We should begin with protecting. The fixer original in mutually dependent reasoning is where one individual wants to fix others' concerns like it's their work throughout everyday life. At the point when that is your psyche's propensity then, at that point, it's extremely helpful to find a BFF who needs constant protection and who rests on you to deal with their life and their brain for them. The other way around, on the off chance that you don't put stock in that frame of mind to mind your psyche, to settle on your own choices, to conclude what you need without another person endorsing it on the off chance that you're not getting a sense of ownership with your life, it's so comfortable to find a BFF who is glad to step in and do it for you.

I'm not looking at needing additional help in a pandemic, after a separation or a misfortune, yet rather the consistent persistent day-to-day or week after week protecting that mutually dependent cerebrums simply love to be on one or the other side of. This prompts a lopsidedness in the relationship in light of the fact that the compromise is off.

Here the provider frequently overlooks their own needs since they are occupied with protecting. The taker keeps on externalizing their lives, trusting and depending on the provider and her perspective more than their own.

This sort of lopsidedness can frequently lead the provider to put your companion's needs and needs in front of your own, and the taker to put the provider's perspective and inclinations in front of their own, which is at the center of mutually dependent reasoning. This frequently comes from and prompts an absence of limits and cutoff points where one individual's necessities wear the pants. In one or the other job, you're enmeshed to such an extent that dealing with another person replaces dealing with yourself.

It's a good idea that in a mutually dependent fellowship you:

concur with your companion when you don't really concur with her

you tell her she's right when you somewhat think she wasn't

shift focus over to them to guide you, think, feel, and express as opposed to checking in with yourself first dump on him without inquiring as to whether he has the profound space to hear it since you accept he causes you generally do

go with decisions for your own life depends more upon what your companion needs than what you need

Sensibly these prompts combined as one feeling, where our wonderful regular human sympathy gets mistaken for the longing to be preferred and respected. Through this cycle, you forget about what YOU feel and what THEY feel. It gets generally confused in this way, step by step, you are less associated with yourself and your own convictions and truth.

From this close-to-home enmeshment, it feels like testing to maintain that should what you like to do when your companion believes should accomplish something else.

You feel regretful for needing to go through the night alone, for needing to take a walk when she has spasms, and believe you should lounge chair it and watch a film with her.

You feel remorseful when you begin dating since you invest less energy with your companion.

You stress over having various conclusions that your companion probably won't concur with - like that perhaps her manager is correct and it's not only that he's a jerk.

Or on the other hand, her accomplice truly isn't dealing with her well and you might want to share your contemplations about it. Yet, you're so stressed over disturbing or losing her that you keep quiet and keep down a piece of yourself to individuals who please her without acknowledging you're making it happen.

At the point when two individuals are so profoundly enmeshed, envy is normal. Another companion, date, side interest, or occupation feels like a danger to your wellspring of approval.

Companionship can get controlling when one companion feels compromised.

At last, this one is a major warning for me, and my clients name this one frequently - feeling just depleted in the wake of investing energy with your companion. You're being approached to give more than you're ready to and you don't define sound limits in view of the enmeshment and human satisfaction.

While hanging out is definitely not a sound to and fro of help, love, and care yet rather, you're endlessly giving. Or on the other hand, you're dependent on that giving as opposed to glimpsing inside and talking about your necessities, obviously, you're cleared out! That appears to be legit.

I love giving - it genuinely gives me such a lot of pleasure to help out - and it must be adjusted vigorously in my life and connections.

In a cherishing, strong together, reliant companionship there should be harmony between compromise.

Not simply set jobs that don't adapt to individual requirements.

Assuming this is reverberating for you yet you're as "I don't do this in my kinships, yet I thoroughly do the entirety of this at work or with my mother... " then apply what you've heard and the solutions for follow here.

How about we talk cures:

Mindfulness, acknowledgment, and activity are the ticket!

Mindfulness:

I love to stop when I understand that I'm in an example I could do without or need to remain in and I ask myself inquiries like:

How could it get this way?

What were my inside inspirations for appearing in a relationship this way by being the constant taker or provider?

Do I oblige my BFF's perspectives or plans since I really need to or am I making it happen so she'll keep on respecting me? In those minutes where I'm putting her in front of me... do I like me?!

Am I attempting to source my self-esteem by being the reliable one without any requirements? Does having continuous emergencies and requesting my companion's consideration around them cause me to feel adored and dealt with in a manner I'm not accommodating myself?

Am I playing out an old relational peculiarity in one or the other job?

I can answer indeed, indeed, indeed, and yes to all of this from the two jobs without a doubt. For my purposes, the cure was figuring out how to help myself, to deal with my own brain first, and to respect and take care of my own internal youngsters as my most adoring guardian FIRST. Then I could go to a companion to give from my profound flood when my cup is full. I could then request support when I've given my very best to have my own back.

Perceive that in a mutually dependent companionship you depend on one another so profoundly, you source your confidence and adorableness from the other and are consequently placing all your supposed close-to-home investments tied up in one place.

This can be an arrangement for a ton of possible torment. That doesn't mean drawing near to somebody, an incredible inverse. Rather, be defenseless, kind, and close without resting your healthy identity on your companion's shoulders. She must convey that for you, that is your responsibility to take care of yourself, my dear love!

Acknowledgment:

When you have attention to these propensities, you get to accomplish crafted by tolerating that you do this.

Frequently we make additional languishing over ourselves by battling reality. We don't get genuine with what's truly occurring and the effect it's having on our health.

Tolerating that your limits are not spotless and clear is fundamental if you have any desire to define solid limits pushing ahead.

"What action can I take when having trouble communicating with a companion? When I text and call and they simply don't get back to me for days or weeks?!"

If you have any desire to be content and you need this individual in your life, you get to quit judging that individual and their ability and decisions. You get to quit wishing and maintaining that they should be unique. They don't message on a similar timetable as you do. Alright. They could do without going out as frequently as you do. OK. You get to begin with tolerating them, dropping the judgment and genuinely adoring them for what their identity is, not who you maintain that they should be.

From the spot of affectionately tolerating your companion similarly as they are, you can drop your mutually dependent connection to them.

You can request things to move to assume you need something else, and in the event that your companion isn't down as well, for instance, text on the timetable you like, you get to advise yourself that you have choices here. You can adore them as they are or you can quit being companions with them. In any case, being frantic at them for acting naturally? That is not cherishing or good for both of you.

Investigate where you might be doing that, and welcome some more acknowledgment as you deal with your brain so you can allow others just to act naturally. You get to feel as much love as you need to in your fellowships, paying little mind to how the other individual appears.

Activity:

The activity here begins with understanding what you need, and what your cutoff points are so you can work on putting yourself first by defining solid limits and focusing on them. I find it's least demanding to begin with little No's, such as saying "hello companion, I hear you that you're disturbed, however, I'm having an unpleasant day and I`m not going out this evening, I prefer to stay home." At this moment, you can build more self-confidence to stand by yourself and discuss your reality in the whatsoever situation.

I'll state the incomparable Dumbeldore in recognition of Neville Longbottom here in saying: "It takes a lot of fortitude to confront our foes, yet similarly as much to face our companions."

You get to express out loud whatever you think and feel, talk about your requirements, and let your companion appear as the best version of themselves or you can keep on striving in a relationship based on mutually dependent reasoning.

For yourself as well as your relationship to thrive, you get to construct your self-esteem beyond the companionship so you can be your valid self in the fellowship!

Work on asking yourself what you're free for and begin requesting and giving close-to-home assent in your companionships. Before you dump your concerns on your BFF, inquire as to whether they're accessible to catch wind of it. Prepare to hear no, which may completely hurt from the start. That is genuine and it's likewise alright. At the point when you honor your own requirements and those of your loved ones, you'll begin to see when YOU are not genuinely free. Then you can respect when others aren't either and can quit thinking about it literally, cause it won't ever be.

At the point when I'm not free to catch wind of a companion's difficult time, it isn't so much that I would rather not be their companion any longer, yet all the same the very inverse. It's that I love them a lot to say OK when I mean no, which I know is an arrangement for disdain and disturbance. It will make me doubtful to pick up the telephone the following time they call, regardless of whether I feel genuinely accessible.

Sound cutoff points, direct correspondence, and limits are critical to dealing with ourselves AND the connections and individuals we love.

Saying no, it's unadulterated love in real life is not mean.

At times when we put down stopping points where we haven't previously, the other individual may presently not be keen on being our companion. That damages. Let it. Feel it. Accompany it. Then you can go about your thinking responsibilities on it to see that their considerations and sentiments don't have anything to do with sublime YOU.

Then, at that point, you can ask yourself - do you really need to be companions with somebody who possibly needs to be companions assuming you're leaving yourself?

Assuming you understand that you're in either the provider or taker job, recollect that we step into these jobs since they're what we are utilized to. It was demonstrated as far as we were concerned in our groups at the beginning and is what's comfortable as far as we're concerned in light of the fact that it's what we know. Your companion may not actually acknowledge they are giving or taking more than serves them or the fellowship.

This is where we carry empathy to ourselves and our BFF and get strong, in any event, when it's really awkward. We can address the elephant of enthusiastic irregularity in kinship and begin to move things.

From being the taker you can pose more inquiries about your companion. From being the provider you can request that your companion hold space for you.

Match this with figuring out how to deal with your own requirements first. Get out of over-dependence and into association in light of needing to give or get support. Not from the requirements that might be your social standard.

You get to understand that it isn't so much that you will lose companions assuming you appear as yourself. Rather, individuals who actually genuinely love and care for you will cherish YOU for who you truly are.

To be your companion since you appeared in your legitimacy, is that somebody whose kinship you truly care about?

Last yet not, in any event, begin to conceptualize and imagine what a more adjusted and solid association could look like while you're coming from affection first. This implies not requesting that your companion penance their requirements for yours, and not consent to do that either any longer. The more moored you are in yourself and your needs and needs, the more you trust yourself to talk to them, and the more grounded your reliant fellowship bond can be. Your kinship will become further as you deal with yourself first, then second, with adoration.

CODEPENDENT FREE

CHAPTER FOURTEEN

Quit Being a Victim and be Empowered

"Nobody deliberately picks or appreciates being a casualty. However, we can guarantee our power".

Being a "casualty" is normally disapproved of. At the point when I used to hear individuals say they were as of now not a casualty, I had no clue about what they implied. As a matter of fact, a casualty is characterized as a person who has been tricked, hurt, or hurt, because of their own feelings or obliviousness, a lamentable occasion, or the activities of somebody who deluded, cheated, harmed, or killed that person.

At that point, I truly was a casualty. I was seeing someone I encountered orderly, psychological mistreatment, yet because of my obliviousness, I didn't have any acquaintance with it. Many individuals, especially mutually dependent people, are involved with junkies or victimizers, incorporating associations with accomplices or guardians who have a psychological sickness, for example, bipolar state of mind issue or fringe, total disregard for other people, or self-absorbed behavioral condition. They experience the ill effects of incessant and frequently malignant verbal and some of the time actual assaults, double-crossing, control, and different types of misuse that can modify their insight, mental self-view, and capacity to safeguard themselves. Numerous casualties in oppressive connections don't remember it in that capacity, since it's suggestive of the disgrace, disregard, or abuse they encountered in their groups beginning. As youngsters they were unprotected casualties; thus, they didn't foster sufficient self-esteem or figure out how to rise up to manhandle.

There's an expression in Al-Anon Family Gatherings: "There are no casualties, possibly chips in" — implying that when you endure an unsatisfactory way of behaving, you volunteer for it. Discovering that I was obnoxiously mishandled was edifying. Before that, I forgot about excruciating appellations and reactions by defending and limiting them. This is called disavowal. When I confronted reality in a confidence class, I tracked down the words and fortitude to name the maltreatment and say how I had an outlook on it. Incredibly, the obnoxious attack halted, with just an infrequent oversight. I figured out how to withdraw and leave expected assaults before they raised. I was becoming engaged and done acting like a casualty. This interaction required some investment.

They are numerous forms of "Acting like the victim, for example, putting your blames on your work or inaction on the physical or close-to-home situation. The shared factor is putting the obligation regarding your conditions beyond yourself or past your power. Another person or some situation is keeping you from accomplishing what you need.

Learning the Job of Casualty

In opposition to the Al-Anon motto, being a casualty isn't a job anybody needs or deliberately picks. Nobody appreciates feeling weak and irredeemable. There are oblivious powers working that are not entirely settled by convictions learned from the get-go throughout everyday life. For instance, on the off chance that we have a disgraced-based self-idea that we're a disappointment or dishonorable of satisfaction, we'll probably keep ourselves from making progress or joy, regardless of how enthusiastically we attempt.

These convictions are typically mastered by experiencing childhood in a broken family. Oppressive connections are shut frameworks. Frequently victimizers attempt to practice restrictive command over their cooperation with direct dangers or through unpretentious control, like responsibility or sabotaging, to hold their accomplice back from conversing with others or getting outside data and help. Harmful guardians do this, as well, to conceal their disgrace and keep up appearances, by utilizing obvious dangers of discipline in the event that the maltreatment is related to other people, or with adages, such as, "We don't share our grimy clothing," and "Blood is thicker than water." Casualties may not have the foggiest idea that there's a help or how to get to it and may fear for their life or friends and family assuming it's accounted for. Utilizing kids to coerce a mate is entirely expected.

Becoming Enabled

Becoming enabled and leaving exploitation behind is troublesome and incredibly difficult to do all alone. We as a whole are too used to our own viewpoint and tedious idea designs that go unchallenged until we converse with somebody with an alternate, better viewpoint. For example, I felt caught when I was loudly manhandled while riding in the vehicle. Until my Al-Anon support made the idea, I'd never considered escaping the vehicle. At the point when I did, I was unable to accept the prompt, elating, enabling, and freeing high I felt. Had I not talked about the issue with her ahead of time, that activity could never have seemed obvious to me. I began driving independently in my own vehicle to the occasion. Along these lines, I could leave when I needed, keep away from oppressive discussions, and not stress over my accomplice's collectedness. By figuring out how to shout out and define limits, I was becoming enabled and was as of now not a casualty of another person's temperament or conduct.

Moves toward Self-Strengthening

Whether you truly are a casualty in a harmful relationship or see yourself as one in your life, the arrangement is something similar. These are recommended moves toward accomplishing this opportunity, not really in the accompanying request:

- Learn. Teach yourself more about codependency.
- Get support. Support is fundamental. Look for it from a specialist, experienced life mentor, as well as a 12-Step Program.
- Notice yourself. Impartially notice others' unfortunate way of behaving and your response. Does your response cause you to feel far improved or stop the undesirable way of behaving? Do you additionally do the shocking way of behaving? Explore different avenues regarding different reactions, including none, and see the outcome.
- Adjust your way of behaving. Is it true that you are lined up with your objectives and values? What steps do you have to take to be in arrangement?

- Address your issues. It ultimately depends on you, not another person to request what you need and address your issues.
- Challenge your convictions. What convictions do you have and do they block you from achieving your objectives?
- Assume a sense of ownership with your decisions. What feels different when you say "I need to," rather than, "I need to," and, "I would rather not," rather than, "I can't?" Assuming liability assists you with tolerating your decisions and starts the chance for change.
- Make a move. Get the essential abilities and assets to accomplish your objectives. For instance, assuming you've been pestering your accomplice to fix or clean something and s/he persistently won't meet your solicitation, either get what it takes to do it without anyone's help or recruit somebody who will. On the off chance that an absence of preparation or training prevents you from chasing after a vocation you need, pursue the essential classes regardless of whether it will require quite a long while.

- Figure out how to be confident. This engages you to be real, put down certain boundaries, and fabricate your confidence.
- Try not to fault or be protective. Assume a sense of ownership with your joy, misery, and your part in conflicts and issues in your relationship, whether your accomplice does likewise. Offer to set things right for your commitment.

CHAPTER FIFTEEN

How to Stop Falling In-love for The Wrong Person

Assuming you are observing that you are going gaga for some unacceptable individual, this is reasonably something you might want to change. There are ways of doing this. Peruse this chapter to study what you can do, so you'll have a superior possibility of tracking down the ideal individual for you.

Could you at any point go gaga for some unacceptable individual?

Falling head over heels for some unacceptable individual is something that can happen to anybody. You might have seen somebody and needed to get to know them, and you wound up dating and became hopelessly enamored.

This doesn't mean they are the ideal one for you. There are many signs en route that could have let you know what sort of an individual they are, and you overlooked them. Assuming the accomplice you are with has done things that you could do without or once in a while acted unsuitably, this might mean you are dating some unacceptable individual.

What happens when you go gaga for some unacceptable individual?

In the event that you experience passionate feelings for some unacceptable individual, you might be seeing someone whose necessities are going neglected. They may not be treating you well, or you may be placing more into the relationship than the other individual is.

This could prompt you to feel despondent or overlooked, influencing your self-esteem. Assuming you have low self-esteem, you may not feel like you truly deserve somebody cherishing you. This isn't accurate, notwithstanding.

Remember that occasionally it's smarter to be distant from everyone else than from some unacceptable individual, particularly assuming your accomplice treats you such that makes you anxious. The point when you are without help from anyone else allows you an opportunity to dive more deeply into your preferences and interests.

For what reason would we say we are drawn to some unacceptable individual?

There are a couple of reasons you might be picking some unacceptable individuals. You could feel like you're not deserving of affection or that the manner in which you are getting treated by an individual is what you merit. Once more, you should chip away at your confidence and self-esteem assuming you wish to change this.

Next time you can't help thinking about why I continue to pick some unacceptable man, contemplate what these men share practically speaking. Assuming they mistreat you or can't accommodate your feelings, it very well might be an ideal opportunity to find a mate that will cure these issues for you.

You should consider on the off chance that you are in a solid relationship assuming that you became hopelessly enamored with some unacceptable individual. A sound matching will have trust, and major areas of strength, and you will have a solid sense of security and regard too. In the event that you don't see these characteristics in your relationship, you ought to conclude how you need to change things.

Look at this video for additional subtleties on why you could be drawn to some unacceptable individual.

Ways of halting succumbing to some unacceptable individual all the time:

At the point when you are making an honest effort to quit succumbing to some unacceptable individual, these tips might have the option to help. On the off chance that you are fed up with requesting that you how to move past some unacceptable individual, this might be a rundown you want to take notes on.

1. Recognize the truth about individuals

At the point when you find you are succumbing to some unacceptable individual, you want to ensure that you recognize the truth about somebody. They might be appealing and direct decent sentiments toward you, yet do they deal with you like their equivalent too?

Ensure that you're not glossing over your relationship. On the off chance that there are things that don't feel right to you, speak the truth about them.

2. Try not to allow your depression to direct your connections

On occasion, you might be falling head over heels for some unacceptable individual since you are feeling desolate. This occurs, and you don't need to thump yourself about it. Simultaneously, you ought not to be seeing someone since you are desolate.

All things considered, set aside some margin to figure out what your identity is and what you like. This will be useful when the right accomplice goes along.

3. Sort out what you need for yourself

It is likewise really smart to sort out what you need for yourself. At the end of the day, figure out what you need and need out of a relationship. Cease dating individuals that won't meet the imprint for you or are reluctant to think twice about you, you are both ready to get what you need.

At the point when your accomplice won't allow you to have your direction now and again, and everything is uneven, this is the manner by which to be aware assuming that you're with some unacceptable individual. A person who regarded you would be fair.

4. Work on your confidence

Since your confidence might be the explanation you think, "I went gaga for some unacceptable individual," this is the sort of thing that you ought to chip away at. In the event that you have experienced past injury or misuse, it tends to be valuable to work with a specialist about these issues.

Exploiting treatment of this kind can have an effect on the way you approach different circumstances and help with leveling up those feeling skills about yourself.

5. Abstain from attempting to change yourself

You ought to never attempt to change yourself when you are seeing someone. On the off chance that you don't have the foggiest idea of what you like and aversion, learning new things, even while dating someone is alright.

Be that as it may, when you love some unacceptable individual, it could be harder to know your inclinations, and you may be more centered around what your accomplice likes. In an equivalent relationship, the two players ought to do things that they like.

One individual shouldn't direct all that the other individual can do and where they can go.

6. Try not to attempt to transform others all things considered

You shouldn't attempt to transform another person all things considered. Assuming you wind up adoring some unacceptable individual, you may not see immediately that there are qualities they display that you could do without.

As of now, it is impossible that they will change these parts of their character. At the point when you notice that you can't manage a portion of these things any longer, you really want to figure out what you believe should do about the circumstance.

Are the activities you can look past, or would you like to cut off your friendship?

7. Recall that activities are more impressive than words

When you end up being with some unacceptable individual, you could feel that in the long run, everything will be OK. Maybe they say that they will chip away at things that you could do without, or they guarantee that they will treat you better.

You should recall that activities are more impressive than simply words. On the off chance that your accomplice has guaranteed, they would get things done for you and they never followed through on them, this is something for you to consider.

8. Realize that you can have a good time alone as well

You needn't bother with an accomplice to have a good time. In the event that you're not at present dating somebody, it very well might be a brilliant chance to gain some new useful knowledge or begin a side interest. You can likewise do whatever it may take to address your well-being and health.

At the point when you are zeroing in on bettering yourself, you presumably will not have a lot of opportunity to stress over dating. Also, it might keep you from experiencing passionate feelings for some unacceptable individual since you are attempting to sort out your necessities and needs.

9. Improve those communication skills

At times, you could have to improve those communication skills for a couple of reasons. One is to let your ongoing accomplice know what you need, need, and anticipate from them. Another is to shout out when you disagree with something.

Openness is of the utmost importance in any relationship, so chipping away at this ability can forestall battles and permit you to have your viewpoint heard.

10. Be practical about your assumptions

This present reality isn't similar to a fantasy. You shouldn't anticipate that your accomplice should have attributes that are beyond the realm of possibilities. Simultaneously, this doesn't imply that you need to undercut yourself.

Assuming there are things that you really want in a mate, you don't need to limit them since you are going gaga for some unacceptable individual. Take the time you want to find somebody who is a decent counterpart for you.

11.   Try not to allow dread to keep you with somebody that is not appropriate for you

You may likewise have to chip away at how you converse with individuals so you will not be frightened to talk with an individual you like or need to date.

Regardless of whether you are bashful or feel restless when you are around somebody you are keen on, this doesn't imply that you shouldn't converse with them. This might be somebody that you are viable with.

Connect with a singular you have a keen interest in and see what occurs. After you converse with them, you may not be unfortunate any longer.

12.　　Ensure you are getting something out of the relationship

Customarily on the off chance that an individual is falling head over heels for some unacceptable individual, they will not be getting a lot out of the relationship. Consider assuming that yours is this way. Figure out the thing you are escaping your organization and assume that this is enough for you.

In the event that it isn't, converse with your accomplice and see what they will change or on the other hand assume they mind talking about things with you. Assuming they won't move, it depends on you to conclude what your subsequent stage is.

13.　　Take as much time as is needed to track down an accomplice

You ought to never hurry into any relationship. It requires investment to learn sufficient about an individual to feel OK with them. This is additionally the situation when you will quite often fall head over heels for some unacceptable individual.

At the point when you initially meet somebody, converse with them however much as could reasonably be expected so you can gather significant subtleties from them. Ensure that you are focusing and that there aren't much of issues that you can't help contradicting them on since this can let you know if you ought to be involved with them or not.

14.   Pay attention to your stomach

Instinct is something strong. You might think or feel that you have been going gaga for some unacceptable individual, however, you overlooked it. Then inevitably, you might have understood that they aren't the ideal one for you.

Do your best not to disregard these sentiments, since they could be safeguarding you and your heart from getting injured.

15.   Ask others for exhortation

Asking others for counsel on relationships is alright. On the off chance that you know somebody who has been hitched for a really long time or you have companions in blissful couples, you might have the option to gain a couple of things from them.

Make certain to pose inquiries on viewpoints that you are uncertain about, and they can probably help. Having different perspectives regarding a matter might assist it in sounding good to you.

16.   Try not to go for awful matches

Ensure that you're not dating somebody since you need to be seeing someone. On the off chance that you are dating individuals you could do without or share nothing practically speaking with, you could get injured.

All things being equal, set aside some margin to track down somebody that you like. Going gaga for some unacceptable individual could leave you feeling tainted, and you can't see the perfect individual when they go along. You'd presumably prefer to keep away from this if possible.

17.   Do whatever it takes not to return to exes

You shouldn't run back to your exes all things considered. They are your exes for an explanation on many occasions, and they weren't ideal for you.

You owe it to yourself to see what is out there. On the off chance that you don't have any idea where to go, you might need to consider web-based dating applications, where you can meet individuals and converse with them for some time before you mean to meet face to face.

This can give them an amazing chance to get to know them.

18.   Have your own advantages

Be certain that you know about things you like. On the off chance that you have no interests of your own, you ought to figure out what you appreciate and what satisfies you. There's no right response since everybody's preferences are unique.

Maybe you like to eat frozen yogurt out of the container and watch cooking shows. These things are fine. It is alright to tell your mate these are things you like. They ought to have the option to acknowledge them when you acknowledge the things they do.

19.   Change your dating propensities

In the event that you have been dating individuals that weren't really great for you, it very well might be an ideal opportunity to reconsider how you are dating. Maybe you met your last couple of beaus through prearranged meet-ups.

Reevaluate continuing any more prearranged meetings. You might have better karma meeting somebody without anyone else.

20.   Try not to ask somebody to date you

There may be times when you need to date somebody, and they don't feel the same way. You shouldn't ask an individual to date you.

This is probably not a legitimate method for starting a relationship, and you may continuously contemplate whether they were simply having compassion for you.

21.   Just date accessible individuals

It is never really smart to attempt to date somebody that isn't accessible. On the off chance that somebody is as of now seeing someone hitched, you ought to think of them as forbidden and let them be.

You can't wonder why you experience passionate feelings for some unacceptable individual when you succumb to an individual who can't give you the things you want. Remember this while looking at planned accomplices in the middle between connections.

What do you do when you become hopelessly enamored with some unacceptable individual?

At the point when you are going gaga for some unacceptable individual or have proactively fallen head over heels for them, you need to figure out what you need to do. Assuming you will make it work and penance things that you like and need, this is your decision to make.

You can converse with your mate and check whether you can think twice about one another. It very well might be conceivable.

In any case, when you're not getting the things you really want out of your relationship and your mate isn't willing to roll out any improvements, you ought to think about different choices.

It very well might be an ideal opportunity to cut off the friendship and figure out more about yourself or begin dating another person. Recollect that there ought to be no hurry to get into another match; you can take as much time as necessary.

Printed in Great Britain
by Amazon

31249549R00112